THE HEART of DAVID JOURNAL

Leading with Vision, Passion, and Wisdom.

VOLUME 1

by David Mayorga

Published by

SHABAR PUBLICATIONS
www.shabarpublications.com

Most Shabar Publications products are available at special quantity discounts for bulk purchase for sales promotions, fund-raising and educational needs. For details, write Shabar Publications at mayorga1126@gmail.com.

The Heart of David Journal Volume 1
Leading with Vision, Passion, and Wisdom
by David Mayorga

Published by Shabar Publications
3833 N. Taylor Rd.
Palmhurst, Texas 78573
www.shabarpublications.com

This book or parts thereof may not be reproduced in any form, stored in a retrieval system, or transmitted in any form by any means - electronic, mechanical, photocopy, recording, or otherwise - without prior written permission of the publisher, except as provided by United States of America copyright law.

Unless otherwise noted, all Scripture quotations are from the New Kings James Version of the Bible. Copyright@1979, 1980, 1982 by Thomas Nelson, Inc., publishers. Used by permission.

Copyright @ 2017 by David Mayorga
All rights reserved

ISBN: 978-0-9991710-3-5

Contents

Preface 6

Chapter 1: What Are You Becming in the Process? 8

Chapter 2: Let Others Sleep and Slumber - Not You! 10

Chapter 3: The Best Way to Guard Your Heart and Mind! 12

Chapter 4: Don't Be Frightened, Not Even for a Moment! 15

Chapter 5: Stop Wishing and Start Doing! 17

Chapter 6: Secrets to Abundance! 20

Chapter 7: Bridge-Makers! 22

Chapter 8: The Storm is Here - How Would You React? 24

Chapter 9: Your God-Crafted Design:
The Fire Behind Your Passion! 26

Chapter 10: God's Vision:
The Fire Behind an Intentional Life! 28

Chapter 11: That You May Know! 31

Chapter 12: No Results - Why Not? 34

Chapter 13: Why Have You Settled For So Little? 37

Chapter 14: The Value of An Open Heaven! 40

Chapter 15: A Brightened Countenance! 43

Chapter 16: Worldly Greatness vs. Kingdom Greatness 46

Chapter 17: Enter Into His Rest! 49

Chapter 18: Smooth Stones! 52

Chapter 19: The Awesome Benefit of Letting Go! - Part 1 55

Chapter 20: The Awesome Benefit of Letting Go! - Part 2 58

Chapter 21: The Awesome Benefit of Letting Go! - Part 3 61

Chapter 22: The Splendor of His Thoughts! 64

Chapter 23: Don't Abort the Countless Possibilities
Hidden in God's Word 68

Chapter 24: Christmas Or Mas de Cristo? 71

Chapter 25: Getting the Attention of God! 73

Chapter 26: Believe with the Heart and Do It! - Part 1 76

Chapter 27: Believe with the Heart and Do It! - Part 2 78

Chapter 28: Believe with the Heart and Do It! - Part 3 80

Chapter 29: No Wonder the Proud Never Win! 83

Chapter 30: Unholy Hesitation! 86

Chapter 31: It's Getting Windy Out There! 89

Chapter 32: Are You Aware of What God is Doing
In Your Life? 93

Chapter 33: A Portrait of the Slothful Servant 96

Chapter 34: The Unlimitedness of God! 99

Chapter 35: One Thing Is Needed! 101

Chapter 36: The Secret of Increase! 104

Chapter 37: Too Busy to Worship? 107

Chapter 38: Wake Up! Class Is In Session 110

Chapter 39: Don't Get "Wowed" by What You See! 113

Chapter 40: God Will Bring Us Full Circle! 115

Chapter 41: When Good Things Start to Come In Bunches Upon You! 118

Chapter 42: Beware of the Spirit of Slumber! 120

Chapter 43: The Diligent! 123

Chapter 44: The Jacob in All of Us! 126

Chapter 45: Flourish Where You *Presently* Are! 130

Chapter 46: Why Am I Being Stirred Within? 133

Chapter 47: Why God Wants to Take You for a Ride! 135

Chapter 48: Follow God's Picture for You 138

Chapter 49: Keep Holding-On Till God Steps In! 140

Chapter 50: The Art of Listening Diligently to the Sound that Instructs 143

Chapter 51: The House of God ! 145

Chapter 52: As You Go! 148

For More Books 152

Preface

He also chose David His servant, and took Him from the sheepfold; from following the ewes that had young He brought him, to shepherd Jacob His people, and Israel His inheritance. So he shepherded them according to the integrity of his heart and guided them by the skillfulness of his hands." (Psalm 78:70-72)

When I began writing this book, it was to provide and facilitate practical, everyday biblical truths that would inspire and motivate God's servants in every realm of their personal lives.

Having served Jesus for at least 30 years of my life and been involved in the ministry of the Word to equip and train God's servants, it didn't take me long to realize that one of the greatest needs in the body of Christ is practicality.

Most believers tend to fall into complacency and become enamored with the idea of simply "receiving" from the ministry they are under.

After church meetings, believers tend to drop the sword and shield as they unpreparedly head to the workplace, not knowing how to fight and possess all that God has for them.

I heard a man once say that believers were "so spiritually-minded that they were of no earthly use!" From what I have personally seen and heard, this statement couldn't be more accurate.

In the day we presently live in, the church makes its loudly boasts on how much they pray and fast and study God's Word yet in all this boasting I must ask where is the power and testimony of the life of Jesus at work in our lives, homes, vocation, and/or ministries?

It is with this heart that I come to you in these writings, providing revelation, knowledge, and present-day truth to our daily lives.

I still believe that we, as believers, are responsible for grasping God through prayer and fasting; we are responsible for hearing His will and quickly obeying and walking out the revelation He has given.

Finally, we are to release through brokenness of heart and contriteness of spirit, the glory which God has deposited within us until **"the earth be filled with the knowledge of the glory of the LORD, as the waters cover the sea."** (Habakkuk 2:14)

May the Lord use these writings to enrich, empower, and enable your life to a more fruitful walk with Jesus.

David Mayorga, *Author*

1

What Are You Becoming in the Process?

"The word which came to Jeremiah from the Lord, saying: "Arise and go down to the potter's house, and there I will cause you to hear My words." Then I went down to the potter's house, and there he was, making something at the wheel. And the vessel that he made of clay was marred in the hand of the potter; so, he made it again into another vessel, as it seemed good to the potter to make." (Jeremiah 18:4)

To say that most of us human beings don't face any issues, trials, difficulties, or opposition in our lives would be an understatement. Most of us deal with various things in our lives, sometimes simultaneously. Adversity is perhaps one of the best tools to develop the natural person; it is one of God's primary tools to separate men from boys and women from girls.

In adversity, we all will have many opportunities to become more significant and discover how frail, weak, and needy we can be. So, my question is – what are you becoming in the process of adversity? What is the function accomplished in your life? Let's evaluate.

First, let's take a closer look at the process. The process is the system that our Creator has placed for personal development. It is that thing that unveils who we are. Have you ever seen a potter at work? Typically, a potter takes clay and mixes it with water to form something worthwhile. Yes, the potter will make it into a drinking cup, dish, or a helpful vessel from dirt and moisture.

Now, picture the clay forming into something precious on the potter's wheel. Round the wheel goes – water is poured on the clay to keep it pliable and easy to work with. The potter knows precisely where he is going with this project, but the clay doesn't know where or what it is becoming. This is often the feeling we get when our life seems to be going in circles. Have you been there?

People will come and ask us, "How are you doing?" Most of us say we are 'doing well' even when we are not. As clay sitting on the potter's wheel, we make every effort not to complain, to stay put, and pray to God that we don't do something crazy during the process.

The secret of champions lies in their vision of becoming. They see the potter working and discipline themselves for the long ride. What an incredible secret this is. They believe their lives are being developed and thus hold on for dear life, trusting God with the outcome.

Let me ask, "What are you becoming in the process?" Are you presently suffering through a vicious cycle of defeats and discouragements? Have you become better or bitter because of the endless circles you have taken while sitting on the potter's wheel? Can you see the potter's hand working ever so intently in your life, making you go deeper in thought, more disciplined in living, and more focused on your philosophy of life? Are you being transformed into something more precious?

Here's what I have discovered: If you allow the process to break you, refine you, and add value to you, then and only then will you be worth so much more than gold! Trust the process and become great. People will come to seek counsel from you not because of what you have done but because of what you have become. Neh'enah.

2

Let Others Sleep and Slumber – Not You!

"I love those who love me, and those who seek me early and diligently shall find me." (Proverbs 8:17)

There is a particular habit that successful people have in common; it empowers their lives and touches every area of their persona. What is this practice? It is called diligence. The Hebrew word for diligence is Shachar, which means "to look early."

The Scriptures are filled with the word diligence or diligently. It is a word that denotes movement bound with sacrifice. The Lord acknowledges those who are diligent and reveals the results of an engaged life.

Why are some people climbing the ladder of success in their own lives, and your own life appears to have been at a standstill for the last few months or perhaps even years? Have you noticed that some things you have attempted to accomplish don't come easily for you, yet things seem to happen naturally and at the speed of light for others?

I am referring to this type of person who learned to climb, work, study, and sacrifice a little more than their counterparts and is now reaping the benefits. 'While others slept,' he was climbing the mountain.

What makes a person of this caliber so extraordinary? Diligence!

A person becomes extraordinary because of their diligence. A diligent person makes choices based on a sound philosophy of life. As I mentioned, "while others are sleeping," he works. Two questions immediately come to mind when I think of such a person: Why and How?

First, let's address the "why."

Most champions are driven by a vision of the future of how life could be if they would only jump in and make a difference. They have so much fire and passion in their hearts that to be sleeping would be a total waste of time. Yet, sleep is needed to refuel the mind and body. So, they compromise and become creative. They awake early in the morning and begin walking out of this vision that burns within. You may find them by their calling around 4 or 5 a.m. Yes, while others sleep.

If you were to ask them, "Why do you get up so early?" They would reply and say, "If you only knew what I was doing, you would rise early, too!" They live in a world of vision and creativity yet remain grounded in their life's purpose.

The second thing is the "how."

What inspires these champions to do a little more than others? What motivates them is the "why" behind their actions and the "how" to make it happen. Creativity is a big part of successful champions; they have formed a habit of being creative. They seek innovative ways to make a meaningful impact.

As you can see, these champions are not just ordinary human beings – they are passionate about life, purpose, and making a positive impact on the world. So, while others sleep, these champions spend their time being creative.

Is it any wonder why they are successful? Do you still wonder why they are living more fulfilled lives? Do you wonder why they live more joyful lives? Don't wonder any longer. Remember: While others slept, they were toiling upward in the night. Neh'enah

3

The Best Way to Guard Your Heart and Mind!

"**Do not fret or have any anxiety about anything, but in every circumstance and everything, by prayer and petition (definite requests), with thanksgiving, continue to make your wants known to God. And God's peace** [shall be yours, that tranquil state of a soul assured of its salvation through Christ, and so fearing nothing from God and being content with its earthly lot of whatever sort that is, that peace] **which transcends all understanding shall garrison and mount guard over your hearts and minds in Christ Jesus.**" (Philippians 4:6-7 AMP)

During my recent meditation and study, I discovered one of the most powerful secrets to a healthy heart and mind. You see, Paul was imprisoned in Rome and was sending the Philippians a powerful letter of encouragement. The words I found are the best medicine for the anxious, worried, and troubled soul.

As I was meditating on what to write this morning, I remembered my visit to a chiropractor and how he explained in detail why my body was hurting the way it was and how my nerves and muscles were continually sore. He treated my body by aligning my skeletal structure and other related issues. My visit was very profitable and educational.

In pursuing God, I have discovered that things work in the same way in the spiritual realm as they do in the natural. If our human spirit is out of sorts or needs spiritual alignment, our mind (soul) and body will reflect the deficiency in our heart.

What Paul writes here is powerful, as it teaches followers of Jesus the secret to staying healthy in spirit, soul, and body.

The Scripture says, "**Do not fret or have any anxiety about anything...**" The Apostle Paul says, "**Do not have anything to do with anxiety.**"

What is this anxiety that Paul is speaking of? How does it infiltrate our hearts and minds? Can it be defeated, and how can we overcome it? These are a few questions that I will attempt to answer in this devotional. First, what is anxiety in this context? Strain varies in degrees, ranging from concern to fear and dread, depicted in both the Old and New Testaments. At the bottom of pressure lies the culprit, the horrendous root of fear.

Most of us have experienced fear at different levels. Some fear has cost us a good life, a promotion, or further development in a calling or vocation. For others, fear has almost paralyzed their lives, preventing them from accomplishing even the most minor triumph.

The Apostle Paul was well-informed about the dangers of an anxious heart to the believer and thus warns us about it.

Now, how does this anxiety find its way into our lives? I believe that anxiety and fear find their way (based on the context of Paul being in prison) through the lack of a healthy prayer life. When I speak of a prayer life, I talk about a prayer life built upon our relationship with our heavenly Father. I don't mean a prayer life based on a ritual born out of guilt and shame if you don't do it. The prayer life, I believe, Paul speaks about relates to knowing God deeply and personally.

Listen to Paul's instruction, "**...but in every circumstance and everything, by prayer and petition (definite requests), with thanksgiving, continue to make your wants known to God.**" You can only make actual requests or demands of someone with whom you have a relationship (this is a compelling truth and principle to abide by). It liberates you by allowing you to transfer your burdens and lay them upon our loving and caring Heavenly Father. Peter said it this way: "**Cast all your anxiety on him**

because He cares for you." (1 Peter 5:7)

After the request has been laid at the feet of God and in your heart, you know He has heard you, and then a celestial peace like a river begins to flow into you. This results from true prayer and a genuine relationship with God the Father.

Paul adds, **"And God's peace** [shall be yours, that tranquil state of a soul assured of its salvation through Christ, and so fearing nothing from God and being content with its earthly lot of whatever sort that is, that peace] **which transcends all understanding shall garrison and mount guard over your hearts and minds in Christ Jesus."** (Philippians 4:7)

God's peace is truly unique. Jesus said that we couldn't find true peace in the world. True peace can only come as a download from heaven into your spirit. Another thing to observe from God's peace is that it transcends all understanding. God's peace doesn't depend on our intellect or earthly idea of what it should be. It transcends our faculties and deposits itself in our very spirit!

The results of an encounter with the living God will kick anxiety and fear right out of you! Paul finishes his discourse on anxiety by saying, "[God's peace] shall garrison and mount guard over your hearts and minds in Christ Jesus."

Paul says allowing God's peace to take its rightful place in you will build a garrison/guard (a protective wall) around your heart and mind. Did you get this? All because you touched the Father's heart! *"Thank you, My Father, for Jesus, My Refuge."* Neh'enah.

4

Don't Be Frightened, Not Even for a Moment!

"And do not [for a moment] be frightened or intimidated in anything by your opponents and adversaries, for such [constancy and fearlessness] **will be a clear sign (proof and seal) to them of** [their impending] **destruction, but** [a sure token and evidence] **of your deliverance and salvation, and that from God."** (Philippians 1:28 AMP)

As I gave my teaching session at one of our Bible schools, I came across this Scripture that stirred me so deeply that I felt the Spirit of the Lord saying, "Expound, meditate, and teach from it!" With this heartfelt cry, I have been motivated to release this principle of truth.

When Paul writes the letter to the Philippians, he is imprisoned in Rome and visited by several of his disciples from the region of Philippi. Things weren't easy for preaching the gospel in Philippi, for there was much persecution at the time. During all this chaos, the gospel of Christ was forcefully advancing.

After encouraging them in his letter to be full of courage and to strive together as an army for the gospel's sake, he added, **"And do not [for a moment] be frightened or intimidated in anything by your opponents and adversaries..."**

For people of faith, the servants who walk and live in the power of the kingdom of God, the Lord says, *"Don't be frightened or intimidated by your opponents or adversaries!"* The enemy gets the message by simply showing your fearlessness and heading to the hills.

I believe God is saying to those whom the Spirit of God leads: Walk in

His power, abide in His presence, and run with His purpose. The minute we doubt, fear or lend ourselves to the devil's lies, we will succumb to him and his tactics.

Fear only paralyzes us and renders us powerless in leadership. We won't be able to lead from behind! Fear, doubt, and unbelief are all enemies of God's destiny for our lives!

Let me attempt to break this down -

Walk in His Power. God has called His children to walk in His power, the power of the Spirit. This is where heavenly wisdom is downloaded, and glorious ideas from God's throne find their way into our hearts. We can rest in His arms once we hear what God says about our life, ministry, or business. Unrest signifies not sleeping in God's endless and limitless provision.

Abide in His Presence. Abiding in His presence is a deliberate choice. We can climb the mountain of God through prayer and abide in Him. We can enter the fresh breath of God and experience His glory as much as we need. Why more believers don't join in is beyond me. I don't know why people don't share more of God in their lives. But here is what I do know: If a man makes his way up to the mountain of God, the Lord Himself will meet him and assure him in all things.

Lastly, Run with His Purpose. As we learn to walk in His power and abide in His presence, we will have the clarity to see and know all God has for us. People drown in darkness because they don't turn on the Light. Confusion, indecisiveness, and overwhelming feelings of despair abide in darkness. Once the Light is turned on, clarity to see and know will come.

No wonder Paul said, **"Don't be frightened, not even for a moment."** The enemy will jump on your fear and paralyze you. In all your wisdom, seek to abide under the shadows of the Almighty. Neh'enah.

5

Stop Wishing and Start Doing!

"He who observes the wind [and waits for all conditions to be favorable] will not sow, and he who regards the clouds will not reap. In the morning sow your seed, and in the evening withhold not your hands, for you know not which shall prosper, whether this or that, or whether both alike will be good." (Ecclesiastes 11:4, 6)

As I reflected on my goals and their importance, I started to think about how often people overlook the value of their present lives, where they are headed, or whether they'll achieve meaningful progress. In my opinion, this mindset is worrisome.

Have you ever been to Disney World? Yes, the place where dreams come true! At least, that was Mr. Walt Disney's vision for the park. The culture you find in this family-oriented park (and now not so family-oriented) is full of dreams. From the moment you walk in, you'll be bombarded with the idea of dreams coming true. They emphasize this repeatedly.

Once you've experienced it, you'll truly believe that nothing is impossible to achieve. It's genuinely inspiring. At the same time, you'll also realize how much effort it takes to turn this idea or vision into reality.

As strongly as you believe in a dream, vision, or plan, you must elevate your life by taking responsibility. Being accountable for your goal means you begin living a conscious lifestyle.

What is a conscious lifestyle?

An unconscious lifestyle is one that says, "I have a dream! I see myself doing my dream! Oh! How I wish it were happening now!" An unconscious lifestyle believes in the dream but, instead of taking responsibility to make it happen, it just wishes. "I wish this would happen!" "I wish that would happen!" or "If only things were different, I could do this or that." Have you heard people talk this way? Maybe you have been guilty of thinking and talking this way.

An unconscious lifestyle means living in poverty across various areas of life. I'm not talking about money or social status when I mention poverty. Instead, I mean this: as you go through life without awareness, your rewards or gains will remain at zero. I'm referring to poverty in different aspects like relationships, health, career or vocation, financial situation, spiritual and emotional well-being, and more.

If you want your vision to come true, you must leave "Wish Land!" You need to adopt a conscious way of living and take responsibility for turning this vision into reality. Many things will change when you wake up and go to sleep, including the opportunities you notice, learning to say "no" to certain things, and investing in something that adds value to your life, among others.

So, what is a conscious lifestyle? This way of living involves intentionally applying key life principles every day to achieve success.

I understand that some people think life will happen no matter what they do. The truth is, yes, life will happen with or without you. The only difference is that you might not like what you get in exchange. You risk feeling sorry for yourself and being very unhappy for the rest of your life. If you don't believe me, look around. It won't be long before you see someone complaining about work, a relationship, an opportunity, a decision, or something else.

Have you ever had a vision but never fully taken responsibility for it? Have you seen someone else envision the future and then make it happen? The difference is that the person who takes responsibility often becomes the owner or leader, while the one who avoids responsibility ends up underneath the one who did.

You're now working according to someone else's vision and dislike it. Who can we blame for this? Can we blame the boss? Should we? Is it their fault that you're unhappy? Isn't it better to look inside and say, "I should move on with my vision!" You won't change your situation overnight, but you will change your course by making the right decision. Eventually, you will reach your desired end.

The magic always happens when you start living according to what you see. Over time, people—family, friends, co-workers, even your enemies—will notice your intentional lifestyle. This is how you live responsibly in every part of your life, practicing core principles, and everything will fall into place.

In closing, don't get impatient when results aren't happening as quickly as you want. Don't act silly or childish – growth is a process! Anything of value always takes time. I call this kind of art slow, steady achievement! Get used to it. It's the life of the conscious. Neh'enah.

6

Secrets to Abundance!

"No man shall be able to stand before you all the days of your life; as I was with Moses, so I will be with you. I will not leave you nor forsake you. Be strong and of good courage, for to this people you shall divide as an inheritance the land which I swore to their fathers to give them. Only be strong and very courageous, that you may observe to do according to all the law which Moses My servant commanded you; do not turn from it to the right hand or to the left, that you may prosper wherever you go." (Joshua 1:4-7)

Often, people don't realize why their lives aren't where they want them to be, while others make a difference with little effort.

In most cases, what sets us apart from others isn't much. We all share a similar basic education in some way or another. Most of us have access to libraries, books, CDs, DVDs, the Internet, social media, and more. We can build a network of people around us, including spiritual, successful, wealthy, and intelligent individuals.

Though many great opportunities for advancement are all around us, why do so many still find themselves "in the same boat" as last year or even three years ago? If we all have equal access to the information needed for success, why aren't more of us reaching it? Does this challenge you? I hope so!

So, what's the difference?

The difference between people who succeed and those who don't usually boils down to three main factors – vision, strategy, and perseverance.

Vision is the ability to see with the eyes of the heart. Seeing a picture of your future is essential for any progress in life. Without vision, life becomes stagnant. Without vision, living loses its meaning and motivation for growth. Yes, people are perishing for lack of vision in their lives. Now, vision alone won't bring you to the finish line. But it can potentially set your life in motion.

The next topic is strategy. What exactly is strategy? It's a list of goals you commit to achieving your God-inspired vision. No matter how many plans you need to follow, write them down and stick to them! Without a strategy, reaching your desired outcome is unlikely. It simply won't happen. People who have a clear strategy are often business owners; they tend to lead richer, more fulfilling lives. They are also the ones who will change and influence the world. You could be next! Goals must be honored by whoever writes them down; otherwise, they won't be effective.

And finally, we have perseverance. The dictionary provides valuable insight into this word. Just listen to this: Perseverance – steady persistence during action, with a purpose or in a specific state, especially despite difficulties, obstacles, or discouragement. The trait of being determined will make a significant difference as you pursue your vision with a strategic approach.

Let me also point out that perseverance is primarily a mindset and attitude rather than a gift or talent. As the vision in your heart unfolds before you and as you write down the necessary goals to achieve it, perseverance will hold onto these things and push through until the vision is realized.

Does perseverance ever stop or pause? Yes! It only does so after reaching its goal.

As I finish this devotion, hear my heart on this: You can pursue your vision and strategy, and keep going until your dream becomes reality. Of course, you can succeed. You can change the world by first changing your own world! Neh'enah.

7

Bridge-Makers!

"And after that many days were fulfilled; the Jews took counsel to kill him: But their laying await was known of Saul. And they watched the gates day and night to kill him. Then the disciples took him by night and let him down by the wall in a basket." (Acts 9:23-25)

Everyone who has ever succeeded at anything will tell you they didn't get there alone. If they are honest, they'll admit that someone helped them along the way. It could have been a parent, a friend, a coach, a teacher, or a professor - it could even have been an angel of God. To everyone who has contributed to your success, I call them bridge-builders.

Bridge-makers are usually selfless individuals who take joy in seeing others succeed in their pursuits. It's rare to find people who truly care about your growth and achievements.

I will outline some characteristics that a bridge-builder possesses. In my experience, these are essential elements in constructing bridges.

Bridge-makers are people who enjoy seeing others succeed in life. They want others to reach their full potential. The bridge-maker is confident in their calling and unafraid to invest in others' growth.

Bridge-makers are people with the vision to help others reach their dreams. These individuals believe in others' dreams and go out of their way to support them in achieving their goals. When someone with a vision gets stuck, the bridge-maker will choose words that encourage, affirm, empower, and motivate the dreamer to keep going until they see their dream come true.

Bridge-makers have a perspective on life that is far more meaningful than their own. They see the big picture and recognize endless possibilities. Most people tend to fail because of selfish ambitions. They fall apart when faced with obstacles and break down under pressure due to egotistical pursuits, but not bridge-makers.

Bridge-makers are people of faith and determination. As natural visionaries, they see the unseen clearly. Achieving their heart's desires isn't difficult because they believe in what they see. So, they keep going until their goals become reality.

We all need bridge-builders in our lives. That's what it means to build a bridge. It could be a concept, a truth, a single word, or just a simple gesture or action done for you; it might be all you need, and it can change your life forever.

As I finish this devotion, I want you to take a moment to reflect on how many people you've helped by building bridges in your life. If you haven't helped someone move from one point to another, it's not too late – you can still become a bridge-builder. Nothing is more rewarding.

My friends, start building bridges if you haven't already. Can you imagine someone on the day of your funeral standing up and speaking of you with tears in their eyes and a broken heart, "He was a bridge-maker. I was never the same after I met him!"

To God be the honor, the glory, and the power forever and ever. Neh'enah.

8

The Storm is Here – How Will You React?

"And after He got into the boat, His disciples followed Him. And suddenly, behold, there arose a violent storm on the sea so that the boat was being covered up by the waves, but He was sleeping. And they went and awakened Him, saying, Lord, rescue and preserve us! We are perishing!" (Matthew 8:23-25 AMP)

Over the past few weeks, I have been reflecting on character and what qualifies someone to be a leader. One of the most notable traits of developers is how we handle adversity.

Adversity is another word for trials, tests, or any conflict that impedes your progress. Many people believe they can overcome anything and often boast about how to beat the odds. But that's until the trial hits them—strikes them!

Nothing exposes a person's emotional, spiritual, and physical well-being like a fierce storm of tests and trials. When it comes to true character, words are cheap. Every promise we've made is meaningless until it's kept. People often talk too much and do too little.

One habit that determines whether you will be an asset to someone or something is staying the course. Can you stay steady when being tossed around? Will you be the last one standing even if everyone abandons the project? I'm not asking you to do this for anyone else—do it for yourself.

Many real-life shipwrecks, whether in relationships, management, stewardship, pursuing your vision, or guiding a team, happen because of poor character development. People tend to follow leaders who lack good character or have none.

As I conclude, picture this situation: You are the captain of a large ship, and everyone on board trusts you completely. You leave the port, and soon after, you're caught in a fierce storm. The ship begins to sway wildly, and the passengers become very nervous; they look to you over the intercom for reassurance. So, what do you do? The captain is you! What words will you say?

Think of your marriage, relationships, business, ministry, or next entrepreneurial venture as a ship sailing through a stormy sea. What will you do? How will you respond? Will you give up and jump overboard, or will you hold onto the steering wheel tightly and say, *"By the grace of God, I can do this!"*

Remember: Don't waste your tests and trials on tears. They [trials and tests] are and will continue to be the most valuable education you will receive in this lifetime. Neh'enah.

9

Your God-Crafted Design: The Fire Behind Your Passion!

"But now, O LORD, you are our Father, we are the clay, and You our potter, and all of us are the work of Your hand." (Isaiah 64:8)

What is passion? Where does it come from? How can you tell when it's flowing and when it's not? These questions come up when trying to find our purpose in life or help someone else unlock their full potential.

What is passion? Passion is like a fire in your soul. It's like a powerful energy or force that flows from deep within you. Now, where does it come from? I believe passion is formed when a person fully aligns with their God-given purpose in life.

For example, some people believe they are called to be shoemakers. If you ever talk to a shoemaker, it won't take long to see that they think shoemaking is the most important thing on earth! They will go on about how amazing it is to make shoes. The same is true for anyone who has found their purpose in life—whether you are a plumber, doctor, secretary, minister, auto-mechanic, manager, owner, carpenter, or anything else.

Now, passion can fade. How? I have learned that power can easily diminish when we stray from God's original plan. Can you imagine a fish in water, happy and full of life? Now, picture that same fish out of its environment. Let's say we take the fish out of the pond — we will quickly see it lose its joy, color, purpose, and passion for living, and eventually, it will die. This is exactly what happens to individuals when we move away from God's original purpose and design.

Years ago, a mentor of mine gave me a book that illuminated this subject. In short, the author advised, Learn to listen to your heart! We will discover what drives us when we pay attention to our hearts.

You see, passion is a neutral emotion. We can feel passionate about many things in life. Now, the man or woman of God who desires to please God must always filter their passions so they don't get excited about things God never told them to pursue.

In conclusion, passion is directly connected to purpose. Without aligning with God's plan for our lives, finding passion becomes challenging. We tend to move from one project to the next, from one relationship to another, never experiencing true satisfaction.

Is it any surprise that our world today feels so unsettled? Much of our discontentment stems from constantly pursuing things that weren't part of the original design of creation for us.

I truly see how my life begins to flourish when passion and purpose come together in my own life. This passion is not only felt deep inside but also visible to and experienced by those around me.

The world will undoubtedly be better because leaders give themselves to their God-given design and set their lives on fire. A great man once said, I set myself on fire and invite others to come and watch me burn! Get filled with passion, and others will be ignited, too! Neh'enah.

10

God's Vision:
The Fire Behind an Intentional Lifestyle!

"And for this purpose, I was appointed a herald and an apostle—I am telling the truth, I am not lying—and a true and faithful teacher of the Gentiles." (1 Timothy 2:7)

If you ever feel inspired to do something, you must do everything possible to pursue it. It will require significant sacrifices to reach your goals. It might cost you time and money and even force you to give up hobbies that don't align with your overall purpose.

Living your life with purpose means you've glimpsed something greater; you've tasted it, and now you must claim it as your own. Let me share some tips I've used to reach my heart's desires and dreams.

Advancement Starts Now!

First, when I initially feel something in my heart, I usually write it down. I've learned not to make mental notes of things my spiritual eye glimpses. I will write it immediately. Mental notes tend to be erased as soon as another idea appears. I genuinely believe this is a vital step if you want to see any vision or dream come true.

Secondly, one must visualize what they see and intentionally set specific goals to achieve that vision. Having an idea and writing it down does not guarantee results; it is only the first step. As Stephen Covey would say, "Begin with the end in mind." Seeing the end before you start makes all the difference in whether you reach your goal.

Finally, you must work diligently and persevere in pursuing the goals you have written until your vision is fully realized. Persevere, persevere, persevere! Once you see it and write it down, you must run with it.

A Slave to Vision

Some people never realize their potential because they give up too soon or feel discouraged by small progress. The visionary person will always stay committed to his vision, living purposefully throughout his life. You might think this is common for everyone; unfortunately, it is not.

One of the main reasons some people struggle to stay on track is that they have only ideas without substance. Pictures are helpful, and they are everywhere. It's not ideas that people lack; it's the source from which these ideas come.

You see, most ideas originate in the realm of selfishness. Selfish statements often reveal an underlying focus on the individual and their interests. "What is in it for me?" is what they ask. It's hard to stay the course when the self is the driving force! For an idea to leave a lasting impact, it must be rooted in the person's vision, not influenced by external factors.

As a side note, vision closely aligns with God's design for you. For passion and fire in the soul, the idea must come from God's plan, not just what your physical eyes see, but what your spiritual eyes perceive.

It's All About God's Design

As we align more with God's design for us, the ideas from that source are limitless. So, aim to discover God's plan, and you'll be able to live with more purpose.

Intentional living contrasts with living passively, lazily, or irresponsibly.

Living with purpose means acting intentionally, with the goal of achieving something. Your vision will continually inspire you! Neh'enah.

11

That You May Know!

"Therefore I also, after I heard of your faith in the Lord Jesus and your love for all the saints, do not cease to give thanks for you, making mention of you in my prayers: that the God of our Lord Jesus Christ, the Father of glory, may provide to you the spirit of wisdom and revelation in the knowledge of Him, the eyes of your understanding being enlightened; that you may know..." (Ephesians 1:15-18)

It was the Apostle Paul's strong desire for the church in Ephesus that they would experience the revelatory realm and have the opportunity to understand the mysteries of God and everything related to growing in the knowledge of Him.

On this journey of faith, I have come to see how God guides us into the kingdom at a basic level, like a kindergarten lesson. Then, through His Spirit, He begins to reveal more profound mysteries that will positively influence our walk.

His Spirit reveals God's knowledge to our spirit. After we receive insight from God, it is up to us to understand and accept the newfound truth into our lives. This is how the eyes of our understanding are enlightened. Through our spirit's eyes, we gain a deeper understanding of God.

Moving Forward by Revelation

While studying the book of Ephesians, I gained a deeper understanding of how God guides his servants from point A to point B, at least in my view. You see, when we lack knowledge, we can't do much. However, when we acquire knowledge and understanding of any matter, we have the advantage of leading.

Leadership, by nature, belongs to those who can see and understand. Seeing is the foundation of knowledge. Once you visualize what you need to know, confidence will immediately be released to your inner self. Speaking from "revelation" carries a different kind of authority than speaking from common sense.

As a servant of the Lord, you have access to the dimension of God's realm. You can ascend to the throne room and wait upon the Lord for fresh revelation on any subject beneath the earth.

One scripture in James says you don't have because you don't ask. If we can't lead effectively, it's probably because we can't see clearly. It's hard to influence others when you play the role of the tail, not the head. Leaders don't lead from behind; they lead from the front with confidence, thoroughly convinced of where they're going, and with a roar.

As I close this devotion, please remember that the leader's call is to be alone with God in the secret place of prayer. Many might think leadership is about competing with others and challenging oneself to see who wins or gets there first.

God's leaders receive instruction in the quietness of His presence. In the world, this style of leadership would be ridiculed. But for those who walk in the kingdom of God and have made Jesus LORD, your calling is in the secret place of prayer.

As you navigate your life, whether in family, business, or ministry, remember that authentic leadership begins with recognizing what God is doing first. The next step is to obey what God is saying.

Over the years, I have come to realize that personal prayer is essential to everything God has entrusted to me. All that I have ever needed —

emotions, strength, vision, assurance, ideas, creativity — is found in the secret place of prayer! Neh'enah.

12

No Results - Why Not?

"When he stopped speaking, He said to Simon, "Launch out into the deep and let down your nets for a catch. "But Simon answered and said to Him, "Master, we have toiled all night and caught nothing; nevertheless, at Your word, I will let down the net." And when they had done this, they caught a great number of fish, and their net was breaking. So, they signaled to their partners in the other boat to come and help them." (Luke 5:4-7)

As I meditated on the experience Peter went through in this part of Scripture, I couldn't help but think about how I have often been in his place. The terrible feeling of working nonstop without seeing any results is heartbreaking. No wonder many give up on their business ventures or ministries, and some even give up in their own lives.

As I reflected on God's wisdom behind this beautiful testimony, I realized that God was more focused on developing Peter than catching a few fish. It was His way of breaking Peter and tearing down his ego.

You might see yourself as savvy and smart in negotiations, but fish don't negotiate. So, what do you do when nature isn't cooperating? Who's in control now? What's your move when everything you know doesn't work? Think about this deeply.

With all my heart, I believe this is God's way of training those He wants to use in greater ways.

Peter's Life Lesson!

Peter was about to learn the lesson of a lifetime — the wonderful skill of relying on God for support.

One of my mentors once told me that gifted people are the hardest to convince that God wants to be their leader. I have both experienced this and come to understand this valuable piece of wisdom. Unless God goes before you, you will never see the end of the day.

Now, there are a few factors that lead to a breakthrough. Let us examine how Peter achieved his breakthrough during what seemed to be an unsuccessful fishing trip.

First, you must allow God to lead in the endeavor. Someone might ask: "Do I have to tell God I'm going grocery shopping?" The answer is "no." You don't have to tell Him you're going grocery shopping. You don't have to tell Him anything; YOU GET TO TELL HIM EVERYTHING!

Whatever "thing" you decide to involve the Lord in, He will be involved with you. If the door isn't open for Him to come in and lead, He won't! Do you understand me?

Secondly, mark the words of Peter. He told Jesus, We have toiled all night. Doing things in our own power will eventually wear us out. Trying to be "God" in all our dealings will also wear us down. We are trying to carry a burden that only God can bear. This will become extremely difficult and, not to mention, very discouraging.

So, what should we do? Listen to God's voice for the need or situation at hand.

He told Peter, "Go deeper!"

Positioning was crucial for the disciples to catch any fish. It all depended on Peter's fishing experience that day. He wouldn't have seen a thing if he hadn't moved into the deep.

There are certain things God has placed into our spiritual being that need the right location and climate to grow. Trying to plant and grow apples in the Rio Grande Valley would be very hard because of the environment. It is too humid and too hot.

Some might try to advance to the next level within the same "first-level" climate, but it won't work. God needs us to move from where we are now; He desires us to go deeper!

Listen to God's instruction for the upcoming season in your life, ministry, or business. You may be fishing in waters that are too shallow. Neh'enah.

13

Why Have You Settled for So Little?

"Then the children of Joseph spoke to Joshua, saying, "Why have you given us only one lot and one share to inherit, since we are a great people, in as much as the Lord has blessed us until now?" So, Joshua answered them, "If you are a great people, then go up to the forest country and clear a place for yourself there in the land of the Perizzites and the giants, since the mountains of Ephraim are too confined for you." But the children of Joseph said, "The mountain country is not enough for us, and all the Canaanites who dwell in the land of the valley have chariots of iron, both those who are of Beth Shean and its towns and those who are of the Valley of Jezreel." And Joshua spoke to the house of Joseph—to Ephraim and Manasseh—saying, "You are a great people and have great power; you shall not have only one lot, but the mountain country shall be yours. Although it is wooded, you shall cut it down, and its farthest extent shall be yours, for you shall drive out the Canaanites, though they have iron chariots and are strong." (Joshua 17:14-18)

While meditating on this part of Scripture, I had never seen vision, warfare, confidence, and perseverance actively at work for someone's desire. These qualities are crucial for progress.

The story above shows how the house of Joseph approached Joshua and expressed their concerns in a respectful way. They explained that their land was too small for them and emphasized how they were a significant people. Their point was valid. They were a great people, and their territory was too limited for them to settle in.

Here is Joshua's statement about this formal complaint. Joshua said:

"If the land is too small for you and you are a great people, then proceed up to the forest country and clear some space for you in the land of the Perrizites and the giants."

Joshua was a leader who commanded with authority and confidence. Leaders don't dwell on what they lack or even consider it. Joshua wanted Joseph's house to recognize their strength and capabilities.

Sometimes, outsiders need to point this out to us in our journey, whether in life, business, or ministry. There is always someone God appoints to share this confidence with us and ensure we keep moving forward. Thank God for His mercy.

The house of Joseph—Ephraim and Manasseh—are trying to move forward without fighting. They had plenty of excuses for not going: **"The mountain country is not enough for us; and all the Canaanites who dwell in the valley land have chariots of iron, both those of Beth Shean and its towns and those of the Valley of Jezreel."**

In natural leadership, people might be tempted to look at surveys and see certain places as more favorable, but this isn't the case in spiritual leadership. Note: We can choose who will lead our lives — the Spirit of God or our flesh.

In spiritual leadership, the Holy Spirit is our guide; if we connect with Him, He will provide fresh vision and confidence to press in upon us.

In God, nothing is finished until He says, **"Well done, good and faithful servant."** Until you hear these words from Jesus our Lord, you are called to move forward, to press on, and to take hold of the land.

Reflect on your life, your business, and your ministry. Has it reached its peak? Can you honestly say, "I have done everything God wanted from me?" Or might part of your discouragement stem from a lack of vision and confidence? Have you lost the fight within you to move forward? Have the struggles of this life overwhelmed you? Have too many obstacles and failures convinced you to stay down where you are?

After hearing their excuses, Joshua proceeded with these powerful, prophetic words: "You are a great people and have great power; you shall not have only one lot, but the mountain country shall be yours. Although it is wooded, you shall cut it down, and its farthest extent shall be yours, for you shall drive out the Canaanites, though they have iron chariots and are strong."

Joshua brought forth the needed words and spoke to them in the house of Joseph. **"You are a great people; you have great power; everything you take will be yours! It doesn't matter what the enemy fights you with; it doesn't matter what their status is; it doesn't matter what weapons they use – the land shall be yours to dwell in!"**

Never settle for less than God's plan for you! God gave you His Spirit to lead you into a life of abundance. It may not be easy. You might have to fight giants, break iron chariots, and cut trees. Just remember that the land is yours if you want it! Neh'enah.

14

The Value of an Open Heaven!

"When all the people were baptized, it came to pass that Jesus also was baptized; and while He prayed, the heaven was opened. And the Holy Spirit descended in bodily form like a dove upon Him, and a voice came from heaven which said, "You are My beloved Son; in You, I am well pleased." (Luke 3:21-22)

When I think about these passages of Scripture and reflect on their importance, I understand more clearly why Christ was such a powerful world-changer. It wasn't His religious background, His outstanding teaching, the many miracles, or even His love and compassion that made Him unique and a force to be reckoned with against all principalities and powers. The key to Christ's life was the affirmation from His Father's voice through the open heavens during a continual prayer life.

An Open Heaven!

What does it mean to have an open heaven?

An open heaven is simply the access we have to God. Everyone can access God, but not everyone takes hold of it.

Let me explain what I mean by not misusing the access one has to God. You see, through the blood of Jesus, we all have access. Knowing we have access is one thing, but entering and sitting in His presence is another. A person must have the right attitude to come and receive from the Lord.

Intimacy with God requires a broken and contrite spirit. You can offer God sacrifices, say repetitive, vain words, or perform good deeds to gain favor, but let me tell you—none of these things matter if your heart isn't broken and contrite!

These are two requirements for experiencing an open heaven. Many pray and even try to spend nights in prayer, but all to no avail! Why is that? I believe that too often, the prayers are not in line with God's will, or worse yet, the servant of God is caught up in self!

You Can't Be Biased Regarding Your Prayer!

This man of God is biased and has already decided what to listen to and do before God speaks. This is a sure recipe for shutting the heavens. No one can see this, but God can. Listen to this: For thus says the High and Lofty One Who inhabits eternity, whose name is Holy: **"I dwell in the high and holy place, with him who has a contrite and humble spirit, to revive the spirit of the humble and to revive the heart of the contrite ones."** (Isaiah 57:15)

As soon as you step into the Lord (assuming your heart is broken and contrite), He will step into you! Think deeply.

I do not doubt that the highway of revelatory knowledge will open when a man or woman of God walks in brokenness and contriteness of heart. The Holy Spirit will reveal the secrets of God.

Don't Block the Highway!

Don't block it or let anything become an obstacle on this highway of revelation. If you focus on keeping your heart open to this highway, you can expect new and fresh words of truth that may influence you both now and in the future.

When God finally speaks to our hearts, it is usually reassuring and Fatherly. Unlike some who think that God comes to shout at us or rebuke us with harsh words, the Father shares information that will build us up, not tear us down. He will correct us with loving judgment and deal with us kindly.

Remember: It is the Lord's goodness that leads men to repentance. "Or do you despise the riches of His goodness, forbearance, and longsuffering, not knowing that the goodness of God leads you to repentance?" (Romans 2:4)

Once you hear His voice, your spirit will be strengthened. Your self-worth will grow greatly, and your self-esteem will reach its peak because the One who created you declares, "You are my beloved!" Neh'enah.

15

A Brightened Countenance!

" And the men of Israel were distressed that day, for Saul had placed the people under oath, saying, 'Cursed is the man who eats any food until evening before I have taken vengeance on my enemies." So, none of the people tasted the food. Now all the people of the land came to a forest, and there was honey on the ground. And when the people had come into the woods, there was the honey, dripping; but no one put his hand to his mouth, for the people feared the oath. But Jonathan had not heard his father charge the people with the oath; therefore, he stretched out the end of the rod that was in his hand and dipped it in a honeycomb, and put his hand to his mouth; and his countenance brightened. Then one of the people said, "Your father strictly charged the people with an oath, saying, 'Cursed is the man who eats food this day.'" And the people were faint. But Jonathan said, "My father has troubled the land. Look now, how my countenance has brightened because I tasted a little of this honey. How much better if the people had eaten freely today of the spoil of their enemies which they found! For now, would there not have been a much greater slaughter among the Philistines?" (1 Samuel 14:24-30)

I've been contemplating this part of Scripture and realized how Israel, during a battle, was commanded to "not eat any food until evening." I'm unsure where King Saul got the idea for this. But after thinking about his order, I probably would have rebelled and grabbed a burger somewhere, especially if I was heading into battle. I'm not trying to be funny or unconventional, but come on! To me, this sounds more like a suicide mission.

The Scripture says that Jonathan (Saul's son) found some honey dripping as he came to the woods. The people wouldn't dare eat any of it, and since Jonathan had not heard his father's charge, he took some honey and ate it.

Now, the results were incredible. The Bible says that Jonathan's face lit up. It transformed him and gave him strength for the battle. Now check this out: **"Then one of the people said, 'Your father strictly charged the people with an oath, saying, 'Cursed is the man who eats food this day.'' And the people were faint."**

I support earthly order and respecting authority, but not when common sense is missing. If any king asked me to kill myself, I would refuse! Maybe you would, but I wouldn't.

Now, there are some quirky things I might do for the gospel's sake, but intentionally getting myself killed wouldn't be one of them, and sitting under certain leadership and dying isn't something I would do either.

Much of what we see in our local churches is nothing more than fear and manipulation disguised as obedience in the name of Jesus. The religious box of our day has significantly damaged the body of Christ. People are still serving Jesus out of fear, not love, as well as out of convenience rather than faithful obedience. The church focuses on minor issues instead of the Great Commission.

King Saul seems like a king driven by fear and manipulation. You can't lead from behind!

Now Jonathan, his son, ate honey, and his face brightened. Wow! Naturally, Jonathan was strengthened and prepared for battle by a bit of honey. Spiritually, honey symbolizes the prophetic revelation from the Lord. You only need a small word to make a powerful impact.

A small dose of revelation knowledge will unlock three key elements for you.

1. For one, it will awaken faith within your spirit, man. This faith will penetrate your spirit and make you come alive. Your spirit, man, will be energized, awakened, and alert to God's power and greatness with in you.

2. It will instill supernatural confidence in you. You will feel that nothing is impossible for you in Jesus' name.

3. It will unleash the courage needed to step into battle. Nothing hinders believers more than a lack of courage. People become extraordinary and make a significant impact because of courage, nothing else.

With a little bit of honey (revelation from the Lord), you will receive a boost of God's faith in you, gaining conquering confidence and giant-stomping courage. Neh'enah.

16

Worldly Greatness vs. Kingdom Greatness

"And Jesus called them to Him and said, you know that the rulers of the Gentiles lord it over them, and their great men hold them in subjection [tyrannizing over them]. Not so shall it be among you, but whoever wishes to be great among you must be your servant, and whoever desires to be first among you must be your slave— Just as the Son of Man came not to be waited on but to serve, and to give His life as a ransom for many [the price paid to set them free]." (Matthew 20:25-28 Amplified Version)

In leadership, it is almost natural to desire greatness for the glory of God. I know some people (Christians, to be specific) who avoid the word greatness in their "religious" vocabulary and insist, "I don't want to be great; I want to be a humble servant of the Lord." As admirable as this sounds, God desires us to aim for greatness. The only issue with greatness is whose glory you are pursuing; whose kingdom are you expanding or strengthening, God's or your own?

Now, there is worldly greatness and kingdom greatness.

Worldly greatness relates to status, reputation, and recognition. It revolves around self and self-promotion. It is an inner drive to be acknowledged by the world and to seek the approval of everyone who sees or hears about you or your projects. It is often self-centered and focused on personal benefit. It aims for praise and continuous approval from others. It becomes a slave to the applause of men.

If a "Christian" leader is not careful with this kind of greatness, they might unknowingly take credit away from God. They may end up building for themselves, believing they are doing it all for God's glory.

Over the years, I have heard many of God's servants say, "I'm building for Jesus!" As spiritual and humble as this seems, the faithful servant knows deep down that these works are often just a way to boost his ego or flesh. I recognize the vanity of these pursuits - I've been there; I know them all too well!

Kingdom greatness depends on humility and servanthood. It's all about serving with a heart full of love. People who practice kingdom greatness are not focused on glory, reputation, recognition, or status.

Kingdom greatness is rooted in humility and brokenness. It involves giving time, money, effort, blood, sweat, and tears. It constantly sacrifices more. Going the extra mile in everything you do is the key to kingdom greatness.

If kingdom greatness had a voice, it would sound like this: "I want to give until there is no more to give! I want to love until I can't love anymore! I want to serve until I can't serve anymore! I fully understand that this life is not my own. I was bought with a price, and now I am indebted to my King! My call now is to know Him and to make Him known until His glory covers the earth like the waters cover the sea!"

Suppose you are a leader and strive to lead according to God's standards (by His Word and Spirit); know that God will honor you in every way. There is no need to imitate others or feel insecure in your business, organization, or ministry. He will provide all the creativity you need to succeed. Learn to walk in Proverbs 3.

Kingdom greatness depends on knowing Christ personally. The leader must base everything on Jesus Christ, the Author and Finisher of all in life. We should not leave Jesus at home while going to our ministry, business, vocation, or work. We need to recognize this. If the Holy Spirit's guidance doesn't go with us in all we do, we are doomed from the start.

Kingdom greatness resides in God's heart for those who love Him. Without the mindset of striving for greatness to bring glory to God, we will become stagnant in our lives. Our testimony will grow stale, and we won't make a significant impact on kingdom expansion. Neh'enah.

17

Enter His Rest!
Learning to Hear the Whispers of the Spirit.

"Come to Me, all you who labor and are heavy laden, and I will give you rest. Take My yoke upon you and learn from Me, for I am gentle and lowly in heart, and you will find rest for your souls. For My yoke is easy and My burden is light." (Matthew 11:28-30)

"Let us, therefore, be diligent to enter that rest, lest anyone fall according to the same example of disobedience." (Hebrews 4:11)

In the original Greek, the word *enter* means "to go or come into." It is commonly used to mean "to enter."

One must step into the Lord to access all that God has to offer. One must "enter" or "come into" the person of Jesus. Entering Jesus is like stepping into a room, and this room is Him! Can you picture it in your mind?

How Do We Enter?

Entering "into" the Lord is a spiritual realization and must be understood as such. One cannot enter this dimension through sheer will. It cannot be achieved by fleshly wisdom or mere understanding. The very Spirit of God guides you in; He invites us or bids us to "come in." We can only enter by invitation!

"Coming into the Lord" is more something that must be understood by faith. It's a two-part process:

1. God dispenses grace, favor, blessings, visions, promises, and more to

everyone who comes and believes...

2. We become direct recipients as we attentively listen to the Spirit's whisper, which guides us with deep promptings to obey Him (whatever the call demands).

After we hear what the Spirit is saying and obey Him accordingly, we step into the Lord. As we move with God's rhythm, taking immediate action on His command will lead us to the place where we have "entered into the Lord," into this beautiful supernatural dimension of God.

What Does God Demand from His Followers?

In the over thirty years I have walked with God, I have always known this about Him: He pays attention to all His creation, but He shows greater concern for those with broken and contrite hearts. No wonder the Scripture says: **"For You do not delight in sacrifice, otherwise I would give it; You are not pleased with burnt offering. The sacrifices of God are a broken spirit: A broken and a contrite heart, O God, You will not despise"** (Psalm 51:16, 17); and in Isaiah 61:2b it states, **"But to this one, I will look, to him who is humble and contrite of spirit, and who trembles at My word."**

For God to look at any man or woman, the recipient must have a broken and contrite heart and spirit. God observes this and sees potential. We need to be led by His Spirit to hear His precious whispers.

How Should Followers Align Their Hearts?

The best way I can express this is by sharing a Scripture that became real to me many years ago: **"Behold, as the eyes of servants look unto the hand of their masters, and as the eyes of a maiden unto the hand of her mistress; so, our eyes wait upon the LORD our God, until that he have mercy upon us."** (Psalm 123:2)

I attribute this spiritual posture to everything God has brought into my life. When God revealed to me the attitude of servants and maids and how they waited for their masters, and how we, similarly, should keep our eyes fixed on the Lord for mercy—whether it's vision, provision, understanding, power, or purpose—my perspective on life changed.

If you wait on Him, success in all areas of your life will be inevitable. Neh'enah.

I want to give all glory to the One who invited me to "come in!" Jesus said, **"In My Father's house are many dwelling places; if it were not so, I would have told you; for I go to prepare a place for you."** (John 14:2)

The Lord told me I believed it, and now I'm experiencing the many "dwelling places" in Him. You can go there too. Enter into Him now! Neh'enah.

18

Smooth Stones!

"Then he took his staff in his hand; and he chose for himself five smooth stones from the brook, and put them in a shepherd's bag, in a pouch which he had, and his sling was in his hand. And he drew near to the Philistine. So the Philistine came, and began drawing near to David, and the man who bore the shield went before him. And when the Philistine looked about and saw David, he disdained him; for he was only a youth, ruddy and good-looking. So the Philistine said to David, "Am I a dog, that you come to me with sticks?" And the Philistine cursed David by his gods. And the Philistine said to David, "Come to me, and I will give your flesh to the birds of the air and the beasts of the field!" Then David said to the Philistine, "You come to me with a sword, with a spear, and with a javelin. But I come to you in the name of the Lord of hosts, the God of the armies of Israel, whom you have defied. This day the Lord will deliver you into my hand, and I will strike you and take your head from you. And this day, I will give the carcasses of the camp of the Philistines to the birds of the air and the wild beasts of the earth, that all the earth may know that there is a God in Israel. Then all this assembly shall know that the Lord does not save with sword and spear; for the battle is the Lord's, and He will give you into our hands." (1 Samuel 17:40-47)

I have been carrying this message regarding the five smooth stones David used to kill Goliath for weeks. It is interesting to me how little David, full of faith, didn't just pick stones but stones that were smoothed out. This symbolizes stones that had been in the water for a long time, transforming.

As I sought the Lord regarding this subject, I felt God wanted me to study the evolution of stones becoming smooth. I discovered some fascinating facts regarding the transformation of rocks or stones when resting in a river.

Most geologists believe that rocks that start jagged become smooth by rolling on the riverbed and through abrasion. Weathering and erosion break more enormous stones into smaller ones. Flowing water causes the rock to tumble upon another and down the riverbed; this is how they are shaped. Strong currents will turn and make the stone slip against another and another. The continual gentle flow of water and sand will smooth the stone out. This is extremely interesting.

Next time you feel that a spiritual current is carrying your life and all you can feel within is a tumble, a crashing, etc., know that God might be working and perfecting you for the giants up ahead!

Notice David and his choosing of five smooth stones. What is God saying to all of us in this powerful story of true faith and triumph? Here is what the Lord is saying to all of God's servant-leaders:

You are the stone that God is working on. You may not understand all the tumbling in your life, but it has gotten you to a place of concern. You are wondering if this breaking of the jagged edges will ever stop. The answer is yes. God is working on you, His precious stone, and make no mistake about it – God will have Himself a smooth stone "by the end of the day!"

What you must know is that God is preparing you for advancement. He needs a smooth stone. Don't worry about the sun rays beating on you; don't be worried about all the sand passing through you as it gently erodes the jagged edges. The firm edges can only break off with the strong current, and God knows this must occur. Don't be puzzled by the rugged falls and drops – the Lord is doing His perfect work in you. Also, don't be concerned that you are lying on a lonely riverbed and no one sees you. The Lord knows your address and will come and get you when

He needs you.

When David needed to defeat the giant Goliath, he reached into that brook and got himself the smoothest stones he could find (he got five of them, by the way.) Here are some thoughts to take to the prayer closet:

(1) Are you a smooth stone yet?
(2) Do you feel God is still working on you?
(3) Have you accepted God's strong currents with humility?
(4) Have you allowed God's waves to work you over and polish you?

Allow the Lord to have His way in you, and you will become valid for the Master's use. Neh'enah.

19

The Awesome Benefit of Letting Go! - Part 1

"NOW [in Haran] the Lord said to Abram, 'Go for yourself [for your own advantage] away from your country, from your relatives and your father's house, to the land that I will show you. And I will make of you a great nation, and I will bless you [with abundant increase of favors] and make your name famous and distinguished, and you will be a blessing [dispensing good to others]. And I will bless those who bless you [who confer prosperity or happiness upon you] and curse him who curses or uses insolent language toward you; in you will all the families and kindred of the earth be blessed [and by you, they will bless themselves]. So Abram departed, as the Lord had directed him; and Lot [his nephew] went with him. Abram was seventy-five years old when he left Haran." (Genesis 12:1-4 Amplified Version)

One of the most consistent characteristics I have observed in people who have advanced and made a difference in society, a company, a ministry, or a family has been the quality of being able to "let go of themselves" in exchange for something more significant; something with more excellent value and more impactful.

This quality typically doesn't run in our human nature. Most of humanity is more interested in their accomplishments, goals, and ambitions. The opposite of selfishness is brokenness.

Brokenness is about letting go of what you want and desire and allowing God to teach you the way, skill, method, and strategy of success for you in life. Yes, all these great keys will open the vault.

The picture left to us in Genesis 12 is one of brokenness. God needed a man, but not just any man. He needed a man willing to be broken and shattered to pieces and let go of his natural inheritance for a wide, unlimited, and more spiritual one.

I recently spoke to an individual who said, "I have been through much breaking in my life, and I can now face just about anything!" I told this dear believer, "The fact that you are telling me how much you have suffered and how "broken" you claim to tell me you don't even have a clue of true brokenness!" He seemed offended at me.

Listen, when God touches a man, they don't typically go around boasting about what has transpired in their life. True brokenness does not need an announcement or a sign signifying how terrible your cup of pain has been! When you are truly broken, there is nothing to say - for you have entered a different realm of humility.

God Had a Different Idea!

While Abraham perhaps had his eyes set on inheriting his father's house, lands, and cattle, God had a different view of Abraham; it was not just lands and cattle but the possession of nations and generations.

What God saw for Abraham had never entered Abraham's mind and heart before. It was a revelation for Abraham, but everything would hang on to his decision in Genesis 12. Would Abraham leave his country and his father's house for a land he knew nothing about?

Let everyone who reads this know that unless we are willing to let go of the past, the present, the natural, the comfort zone, and the present ideas – we cannot advance to God's eternal plan.

Putting the Axe to the Root!

When the Lord sets us apart for a time of revelation, it is to reveal His heart, mind, and eternal plan.

Now, nothing hinders our lives more than the roots. The idea of transplanting our lives from where we presently are to a place we have never seen or been to is usually out of the question. Too many turn their ears off when asked to give something they have long embraced. They don't even care to hear the blessing that will follow them!

The thought of "uprooting" is out of the question, and therefore, make decisions based on biased and natural perspectives.

In the Lord, things are to be spiritually discerned. If a man or woman allowed the Lord to lead, they would be joyful. How many sad, lonely, upset, and angry believers know? Too many? Now, you know the reason why they are like that.

It was important for the Lord to show Abraham this one lesson first - the lesson of "uprooting."

Unless we learn this lesson, it will be challenging to navigate in the will of God. It was important for Abraham to let go of his roots (the ideas and philosophies he had developed since childhood). The day he had come to leave his father's house, his country, and everything he held on to. It would not be easy; nevertheless, it had to be done.

Once a man or woman of God can walk in this principle, following God's will in every area of life will be easier to follow. Once Abraham obeyed God's command, he was ready to enter the next chapter of his life. The Scripture says, **"So Abram departed, as the Lord had directed him."**

Will you follow Abraham's footsteps and enter your next life phase? Neh'enah.

20

The Awesome Benefit of Letting Go! - Part 2

"NOW [in Haran] **the Lord said to Abram, 'Go for yourself** [for your own advantage] **away from your country, from your relatives and your father's house to the land that I will show you."** (Genesis 12:1)

I want to continue exploring this precious truth I found in the life of Abraham and how God spoke to him and challenged him to take a step of faith.

God told him to leave his country, relatives, father's house, and homeland. Notice the scripture I referenced above: the Amplified Version states that if Abraham went, it would be to his "own advantage."

Why Abraham's Move Was Significant

Let me explain why the first act of obedience in Abraham's life was important. The "uprooting" of himself from his environment (house, family, country, etc.) was the key to receiving God's best.

If a man or woman cannot "uproot" themselves from their current spiritual state, they will struggle throughout their lives. One must obey God so they can move into God's best. Jesus alluded to this when He said, **"Whoever does not persevere and carry his own cross and come after (follow) Me cannot be My disciple."** (Luke 14:27)

Notice how "the cross" is key. One cannot be a disciple if one can't carry one's cross. If Abraham couldn't leave his own country, he wouldn't be able to see the promise.

Once the move is made, another opportunity will present itself to you. Since you made the right choice at first, when the second challenge comes, you won't falter. You will follow God's heart without difficulty because you have already dealt with the "uprooting" in your life.

Abraham's Second Challenge

"But Lot, who went with Abram, also had flocks and herds and tents. Now, the land was not able to nourish and support them so they could dwell together, for their possessions were too great for them to live together. And there was strife between the herdsmen of Abram's cattle and the herdsmen of Lot's cattle. And the Canaanite and the Perizzite were dwelling then in the land [making fodder more difficult to obtain]. So Abram said to Lot, Let there be no strife, I beg of you, between you and me, or between your herdsmen and my herdsmen, for we are relatives. Is not the whole land before you? Separate yourself, I beg of you, from me. If you take the left hand, then I will go to the right; or if you choose the right hand, then I will go to the left. And Lot looked and saw that everywhere the Jordan Valley was well watered. Before the Lord destroyed Sodom and Gomorrah, [it was all] like the garden of the Lord, like the land of Egypt, as you go to Zoar. Then Lot chose for himself all the Jordan Valley and [he] traveled east. So they separated. Abram dwelt in the land of Canaan, and Lot dwelt in the cities of the [Jordan] Valley and moved his tent as far as Sodom and dwelt there. But the men of Sodom were wicked and exceedingly great sinners against the Lord. The Lord said to Abram after Lot had left him, Lift up now your eyes and look from the place where you are, northward and southward and eastward and westward; For all the land which you see I will give to you and to your posterity forever. And I will make your descendants like the dust of the earth, so that if a man could count the dust of the earth, then could your descendants also be counted. Arise, walk through the land, the length of it and the breadth of it, for I will give it to you." (Genesis 13:7-17)

Abraham's second challenge was to relinquish his rights. He was the blessed chosen one by God, not Lot. However, Lot first had to choose which portion of land to keep and make it his own "space."

When a man has dealt with his personal "uprooting" and turned his life over to God, he doesn't face the same issues as others. Once you understand this, you don't fight for the things God wants you to have, but only for what aligns with His will. Abraham had no trouble letting go of anything in his life, because he knew God had promised him something more meaningful.

God knew Abraham's heart, and that was all that mattered. After Abraham gave Lot the first choice and Lot took it, **"The Lord said to Abram after Lot had left him, Lift up now your eyes and look from the place where you are, northward and southward and eastward and westward; For all the land which you see I will give to you and to your posterity forever."**

When a greater vision from God captures our hearts, we will never settle for lesser, insignificant things again. Others can have toys, lands, sheep, and goats; they can be first if they want— "I want God's best, God's promise, God's vision as painted on my heart's canvas! Keep everything else; just give me the revelation that God has placed there." Neh'enah.

21

The Awesome Benefit of Letting Go! - Part 3

"Now it came to pass after these things that God tested Abraham, and said to him, "Abraham!" And he said, "Here I am." Then He said, "Take now your son, your only son Isaac, whom you love, and go to the land of Moriah, and offer him there as a burnt offering on one of the mountains of which I shall tell you." So, Abraham rose early in the morning..." (Genesis 22:1-3a)

Once the servant of the Lord brings Genesis 12:1-4 to life, God will continue to elevate them.

Many years ago, my spiritual mentor, my dear pastor, told me while drinking coffee in his office, "David, did you know that God doesn't give us the complete revelation of what He has in store for us? He only shows us a little at a time but increases it if we obey the last thing He asks us to do. Our destiny depends on our obedience to everything He asks us to do. When I heard this, I realized that letting go of whatever God asks me to do is only the first small step on a journey full of possibilities and powerful God-driven outcomes!

The Most Important of All Moves.

The "uprooting" process is the most powerful of all moves; it is the initial step in our obedience (for more insight, read Awesome Benefit of Letting Go! - Part 1). Before He makes any prophetic move in your life, God will ensure that you stand on His ground, not yours.

The second step upward in God is when He challenges us to release external blessings. In this case, it was the land and space for the cattle (which are both external blessings).

Lot was given a choice, and Abraham had to give up his privilege of being the "blessed one." He was confident that God could help Him stand in any situation he faced. So, he blessed Lot by allowing him to choose first. No sooner had they parted ways than God said to Abraham: **"Lift up now your eyes and look from the place where you are, northward and southward and eastward and westward; for all the land which you see I will give to you and to your posterity forever."** (Genesis 13:14, 15)

Abraham was okay with letting go of the "first choice." He had learned the secret of "uprooting."

Letting Go of the Dream of Dreams!

For those who have passed the first and second tests from the Lord, they must prepare for the third test. It involves letting go of your most precious possession, "the dream of your dreams." In this case, the "dream of Abraham's dreams" was Isaac. God told him to sacrifice him.

Why would God do this to Abraham? Let us consider all the effort that went into this: the weeping, the waiting, the mistakes, more weeping, and more waiting until Isaac was born. All this just to hear God say, "I need you to sacrifice him unto me!"

I know people who would prefer to backslide rather than give their most valued possessions to God. You know exactly what I mean.

How is Your Body Language When It Comes to Obedience?

What amazes me is how Abraham didn't hesitate to obey. You can always tell a man's heart by his body language and quick move toward God's will. The Scripture says, **"So Abram rose early in the morning..."** Abraham couldn't wait to fulfill God's purpose; he was eager for the morning to come so he could go and live out God's wishes. Is this your heart? Is your body language showing a desire to fulfill God's wishes?

As I conclude this mini-series on the theme of brokenness, we need to understand the Lord's intent.

Is God interested in torturing us by taking away the things we cherish most here on earth? Or is He trying to teach us an important lesson about letting go of things that are just tools and not objects of worship?

Let us go deeper into His heart and embrace His ways. I believe God's ways are always the best way to follow divine order. Let us be quick to hear and quick to obey everything He says. Neh'enah.

22

The Splendor of His Thoughts!

"For My thoughts are not your thoughts, neither are your ways My ways, says the Lord. For as the heavens are higher than the earth, so are My ways higher than your ways and My thoughts than your thoughts." (Isaiah 55:8, 9)

"Yet to us God has unveiled and revealed them by and through His Spirit, for the [Holy] Spirit searches diligently, exploring and examining everything, even sounding the profound and bottomless things of God [the divine counsels, hidden things, and beyond man's scrutiny]. For what person perceives (knows and understands) what passes through a man's thoughts except the man's own spirit within him? Just so no one discerns (comes to know and comprehend) the thoughts of God except the Spirit of God. Now we have not received the spirit [that belongs to] the world, but the [Holy] Spirit Who is from God, [given to us] that we might realize and comprehend and appreciate the gifts [of divine favor and blessing so freely and lavishly] bestowed on us by God." (1 Corinthians 2:10-12 -Amplified Version)

As I've been spending some much-needed time in prayer and fasting, the Lord gave me some incredible thoughts. He reminded me of how, without His guidance, I don't have anything to go by. Without His leadership, I will be forever stuck.

Now, only some feel this way. This emotion is usually handled by those who have had an experience with the living God and are convinced that their lives were created for something more significant than just making a good living.

The specific man or woman I am speaking of desires God's best. Do you want God's best? If you do, read on.

Man Thinks in Times and Seasons

As Jesus walked on the earth, He confronted many mindsets. He faced the earthly mindset, the religious perspective, the business mindset, and the political mindset, and He spoke of another mindset – God's.

Man thinks naturally and is in a common-sense mode. Usually, if a man cannot "do the math" to a situation, he panics and goes into frantic fear. This is the earthly mindset, which I am almost sure we all have entered.

Now, the secret to overcoming this is not education. You can't be taught this by flesh and blood. As good and gifted a teacher is, the deep things of God can only be caught in the human heart as God unveils it to man's spirit. This is what it means to be "caught up" in God. Have you been "caught up" in God lately?

When man fails to see God or God's dimension displayed before his eyes, he doesn't know what to say, think, or act. Why does this occur? It occurs because those things must be spiritually discerned and applied. It is God's way of saying, "Come up higher, and I will show you the things you must know."

At this point, man will have a choice: he will seek and knock on heaven's door, OR he will disregard the present event, situation, crises, etc., as usual and unnecessary. Consequently, man will find himself under stress and in much turmoil. It begins in the spirit and ends up in the natural. Sickness starts inside and not long from it in the body.

God Doesn't Have a Clock or a Calendar

The Lord is not concerned with a thing's time or date as He is concerned with His purposes being completed. Once something is finished, He moves on with the next thing on His (not my) list.

As for the Lord and His ways, it is evident that God is much greater, wiser, and powerful. He lives in a dimension where His essence is everything. His presence rules supremely, and everything bows to Him.

When God speaks, things are set in motion. When God decrees something, it is done! There are not enough numbers, methods, days, hours, and minutes in His world. Boxes don't exist. Someone asked me the other day, "So, are you thinking outside the box?" I replied, "What's a box?!"

The way God thinks and moves is mind-boggling! He does things without limitations. God is King over time and space. He is eternal - go figure.

God Blew Me Away!

There was a time when I had been praying about the next move in my ministry. I had been renting a location for a year, and the lease was coming up for renewal in a few months. I wasn't sure if I was to renew my lease and continue at the same pace of doing ministry. I took the matter to God, fasted, and prayed for God's guidance.

After praying for a few weeks on this saying, "God, I need a building for my church. Please help me decide my next move. What do you want? I need a building, Lord!" After many days of praying this "whiny prayer," God spoke to me - not with an answer but a question. God asked me, "David, how big of a building do you need to fit a whole generation?" I was speechless.

What the Lord was teaching me was the way He thinks. God doesn't think in buildings but in generations. God doesn't think in goals but in concepts. God doesn't think in ideas but in purposes.

If God is bringing you to a place of stagnation (standstill, confusion, a desert season, adversity, etc.), it is for this very thing. He wants to reveal to you His thoughts. Here's my counsel to you:

1. Write all your concerns on a piece of paper.
2. Take it to God in prayer.
3. Ask Him for His specific thoughts on the matter.
4. Get ready to live in joy and peace in the Holy Spirit.

Neh'enah.

23

Don't Abort the Countless Possibilities Hidden in God's Words!

"Now the men whom Moses sent to spy out the land, who returned and made all the congregation complain against him by bringing a bad report of the land, those very men who brought the evil report about the land, died by the plague before the Lord. But Joshua the son of Nun and Caleb the son of Jephunneh remained alive, of the men who went to spy out the land." (Numbers 14:36-38)

There's nothing like the start of a new year with expectation in the heart and an awakened spirit in the Lord. Along with a list of goals and objectives for the coming year, I also want to add this powerful principle: "Don't abort the countless possibilities hidden behind God's words."

While meditating upon these specific verses, I found a compelling truth hidden in the story of the twelve spies. It was incredible how ten of the twelve spies (due to their fear) didn't enter God's Promised Land. The only two who passed the test were Joshua and Caleb.

Now, let us go a bit deeper and study how fear paralyzes the life out of us.

There are two possibilities when God speaks. One of the possibilities is to believe and reap the benefits, while the other possibility is NOT to believe and reap the consequences. I used to think that following God was complicated, but now I've learned it is up to me to make it work.

If, after God has spoken, we are not convinced, then we are left with nothing but a life of fear, doubt, and unbelief. You would think this was the worst part of our negation of God's words to us, but it is not - it gets worse. Listen to this tragic story: **"Now the men whom Moses sent to spy out the land, who returned and made all the congregation complain against him by bringing a bad report of the land, those very men who brought the evil report about the land, died by the plague before the Lord..."**

Are you reading this? Did you get it? Every spy Moses sent who brought in a bad report about the land "died by the plague before the Lord." In short, God killed them all.

Here is the scary part that fear brings with it. It brings about spiritual death. If there is anything worse than a natural death, it is spiritual death. Can you imagine a man or woman walking with NO SPIRIT?! Not even Hollywood could write such a horrific script!

That is precisely what happened to the ten spies who went to check out the land – they lost their essence! Think about it: a man with no heart. When we choose to fear rather than obey, we eventually die. Then, our life, slowly but surely, loses its zest for living.

In the last few years, I have encountered sincere and honest believers who desire to walk in a higher realm with God. Their desire is pure, and their ambition is a godly one. Yet, in all their seeking after God, they have forfeited this life that God promised because they won't follow God's commands.

I think the church is gravely mistaken when it feels that God will do everything for them, and all they must do is skip and hop over into their promise with little to no effort. I don't think so! Every move we make in God must take faith and action! Never forget this.

As I close this short devotion, listen to this story of victory: **"But Joshua the son of Nun and Caleb the son of Jephunneh remained alive, of the men who went to spy out the land."** The Scripture states explicitly that

Joshua and Caleb remained alive. The word *alive* in Hebrew means "to live; to come to life; to give life." Is your heart burning just about now? It should be!

If we obey God and put off our fears and doubts, God will quicken us or make us alive (to come to life), and then we will be able "to give life!" Do you see the value in obeying God's words and promises? Can you see how our obedience will impact us first and then those coming after us, the next generation?

The next time God speaks to you or shares a vision, dream, or prophetic word, don't be quick to discard it. Some instructions may be hidden within its fiber to take you to your next opportunity. Think deeply about this. Neh'enah.

24

Christmas Or Mas de Cristo?

"For to us a Child is born, to us a Son is given; and the government shall be upon His shoulder, and His name shall be called Wonderful Counselor, Mighty God, Everlasting Father [of Eternity], Prince of Peace. Of the increase of His government and of peace there shall be no end, upon the throne of David and over his kingdom, to establish it and to uphold it with justice and with righteousness from the [latter] time forth, even forevermore. The zeal of the Lord of hosts will perform this." (Isaiah 9:6, 7 AMP)

Another Christmas has arrived, and once again, we are surrounded by the traditions of this special day. Different cultures around the world celebrate Christmas in their own unique ways, and its impact is profound. Jesus Christ, our Savior, is celebrated with food, family, friends, gifts, and sermons on the meaning of Christmas.

These are the times when churches around the world show their heartfelt faith in our Savior, Jesus, and express it through music, pageants, dramas, videos, and other special events. It is truly a big deal!

As I drove down the freeway toward one of my schools, the Holy Spirit began to share His heart with me on this important holiday. I usually don't excel at Christmas subjects; however, I do love the Holiday Season. I love hearing the story of our coming Savior repeatedly. I will never forget to remind myself of how God, the Father, so loved the world that He sent Christ to die for me! Blessed King!

Let me clarify this: Christmas signifies more of Christ!

The exchange of gifts, family gatherings, lunches and dinners, the Christmas tree and lights, the sugar Christmas cookies—oh yes, all of it speaks of Jesus Christ, the newborn King!

Since the coming of Jesus Christ, the Messiah, was prophesied by the Prophet Isaiah (over seven hundred years before Christ was even born), we learn about God's purpose in sending His Son Jesus. Let us examine it:

1. "**...the government shall be upon His shoulder...**" This highlights establishing God's Kingdom within the human heart. Jesus came to reign in the human spirit. You and I are part of a kingdom that can never be shaken. We are now soldiers under His command. He is the Lord, and we are the sheep of His pasture.

2. "**...His name shall be called Wonderful Counselor, Mighty God, Everlasting Father** [of Eternity], **Prince of Peace...**" When Jesus enters the human heart, He immediately becomes your Counselor [wisdom], your Mighty God [you might], your [Father], and your [Peace]! This is one reason we say the world needs Jesus! He fills all the empty spaces within the human heart. To God be the glory now and forever.

3. "**...Of the increase of His government and peace, there shall be no end...**" Being filled with the blessings Christ has come to bring into our hearts and continuing to grow in it, from glory to glory, is the very essence of the Christmas holiday. If we dare to believe in the increase of His government and peace, there shall be no end. The more we hunger to be filled with His Holy Spirit, the greater our longing for more of Jesus. Let us stay thirsty, my friends!

Let this holiday season be the most special yet. Let the Lord renew you in His love and passion. Ask God to fill you with MAS [more] of Himself today, along with greater wisdom and strength, accompanied by an ever-increasing sense of adoption and never-ending peace. Neh'enah.

25

Getting the Attention of God!

"And when Jesus had re-crossed in the boat to the other side, a great throng gathered about Him, and He was at the lakeshore. Then one of the rulers of the synagogue came up, Jairus by name; and seeing Him, he prostrated himself at His feet and begged Him earnestly, saying, my little daughter is at the point of death. Come and lay Your hands on her, so that she may be healed and live. And Jesus went with him; and a great crowd kept following Him and pressed Him from all sides [so as almost to suffocate Him]." (Mark 5:21-24)

What a tremendous story Mark left us and an even more remarkable testimony for Jairus, one of the rulers of the synagogue. Who said leaders don't need God?

You can be a leader with great skill and talent. You can have charisma and status, but character sets a leader apart from others. Yes, mainly a contrite and broken humble heart.

In the story above, Jairus learns that Jesus is in town and, with an urgent need, makes his move. I want you to notice something here: the secret to getting God's attention. Let us learn from Jairus...

First, Jairus didn't care that he was a ruler in the synagogue. It didn't matter to him if people were watching or might criticize him. Jairus moved and stepped in front of Jesus!

Here is the first key to catching God's attention: **"When Jairus saw Him..."** We all see Christ, but for many of us, it doesn't stir anything inside; it doesn't move us either way. Our view of Christ is frozen and lifeless. We see Him, and it doesn't draw us closer to Him.

The Bible says that Jairus saw Him and **"prostrated himself at His feet and begged Him earnestly..."** If this doesn't get God's attention, then I don't know what does.

Most prayers go unanswered because we don't get God's attention. We don't see Him, and if we catch a glimpse of Him, we don't worship Him. True worship is about opening our hearts, kneeling down, and praising Jesus' feet!

There must be worship first in all our asking and pleading with God. Are we getting God's attention by falling at His feet? Or do we think God is stopping just because we say we have a need? Come on! Who are we fooling?

Just Worship!

During personal prayer in the early morning hours, I like to enter His presence with worship. I don't ask for anything or make any requests; I fall prostrate before Him and express to Him countless feelings in my heart about what He means to me.

After adoring Him, I follow whatever the Spirit guides me to do. Whether it's prayers of confession, petitions, or intercessions, my work is already done while I worship His holy Name!

Worshipping Jairus' Way.

Jesus couldn't go anywhere because Jairus held onto Him tightly with his worship. As Jesus looked at Jairus, He said, **"...my little daughter is at the point of death. Come and lay Your hands on her so she may be healed and live."** How can our amazing King of Kings ignore this man? How can Christ ignore a man who has thrown himself at His feet with such earnestness? Do you see what I am saying? The true calling of every man or woman of God is to worship first.

My dear friends, God will never turn a deaf ear when we fall at His feet, and He will not ignore us or tell us to step aside. No sir! Our faith and brokenness will move Him! When we get His full attention, He will respond accordingly. Neh'enah.

26

Believe with the Heart and Do It! - Part 1
Critical Factors in Visionary Leadership

"They then said, "What are we to do, that we may [habitually] be working the works of God? [What are we to do to carry out what God requires?]" Jesus replied, "This is the work (service) that God asks of you: that you believe in the One Whom He has sent [that you cleave to, trust, rely on, and have faith in His Messenger]." (John 6:28, 29 AMP)

When we discuss the works of God, many expect a miracle to occur, or even assume that God's actions are similar to parting the Red Sea, crossing the Jordan River, or causing the walls of Jericho to fall. But are these truly the works of God, or are they the result of someone placing their love, trust, and complete confidence in God for miracles to happen?

"I Believe!"

Interestingly, many people claim to have faith and even boldly say, "I believe," but their promises never seem to materialize or show any sign of their so-called God-given dream. Why do you think this is?

Again and again, I have heard many believers cry out, "I don't know why I don't seem to get out of this rut!" "For years, I have been praying and believing for something to happen, but nothing good comes my way." Does this sound familiar to you? Have you ever felt like God was not on your side, yet in the lives of others, things flow smoothly?

Why do some people feel like everything is impossible? It's like a shadow of darkness hangs over them. They try repeatedly, but nothing changes. They fast, pray, read God's Word, and attend conferences and spiritual gatherings, but nothing happens in their lives!

At the same time, in other people's lives, everything appears to come easily; they seem to be in the right place at the right time, and everything goes smoothly for them! Their world feels full of endless possibilities. Once again, everything they desire seems to slip through their fingers!

It's Truly a Matter of Faith!

Before I start this series, let us reflect on faith and what a heart full of it can accomplish.

Listen to the words of Jesus: **"Truly I tell you that if anyone says to this mountain, 'Be lifted up and thrown into the sea,' and has no doubt in his heart but believes that it will happen, it will be done for him."** (Mark 11:23). This verse undoubtedly holds the key to God's miracle-working power flowing in your life.

If God's power starts flowing into your life because of your faith, nothing will be impossible for you. The works of God are connected to God's faith working in you and through you!

The Basics of Faith

For faith to activate in your life, you must have NO DOUBT in your HEART and BELIEVE that it will happen just as you have believed! The key to belief is that it must be rooted in the heart, not just the mind.

Years ago, I came across a quote: "You don't get what you want; you only get what you believe in!" I believe in this principle.

I pray that your visionary leadership will rise to a new level in God. May your life be filled with God's faith so you can positively and creatively influence your world. Neh'enah.

27

Believe with the Heart and do It! - Part 2
Critical Factors in Visionary Leadership

"Truly I tell you that if anyone says to this mountain, 'Be lifted up and thrown into the sea,' and has no doubt in his heart but believes that it will happen, it will be done for him." (Mark 11:23).

Last week, I started building this study and mentioned that it is essential for the leader to believe with his heart if he is ever to accomplish God's purposes in his life. Anything that comes from the Lord must be spiritually discerned; for that, it requires faith—the faith of God.

Anything that God reveals to us through His Word or His Spirit must be received by God's faith.

There are too many people with bright ideas, but what's needed is not ideas; it's a touch of God that the leader requires. Every touch of God comes through revelation. Too many believers and preachers are running around teaching metaphysical ideas that lack the power of God.

The foolish idea that confessing something with your mouth will make it happen is one of the biggest distortions in the gospel of Jesus Christ in modern times.

Believing with the Heart!

Years ago, I heard a man of God say, You don't get what you want; you can only get what you believe!

There is a formula behind this; it's not just unconscious belief or some alignment of the stars. God has established a law that, when believed in and honored, will bring you powerful, life-changing experiences.

Believing involves NOT doubting in the heart. Whatever download you receive from God, accept it and act on it immediately unless the Lord specifically tells you to wait for a set time. This is how miracles happen. The opposite would be to receive guidance from the Lord and never follow through – then naturally, nothing occurs.

Is what God is saying true?

Doubt kills any word, promise, vision, or idea from the Lord. The word *doubt* means, in its original sense, "to distinguish; to judge." In other words, when we doubt, we distinguish or judge whether God's words are valid. Very interesting.

As I studied this, I see how doubt arises. Remember, doubt is a fruit of the flesh. The flesh will challenge and reject anything related to God. If faith doesn't quickly take hold of what God says, the flesh steps in and drowns out God's wishes!

Now, if we act in faith (the confidence that God has given us, trusting that He is supporting us in our decision), the task will be accomplished! Wow! That sounds too simple. Well, it sounds simple, and it is simple.

More of Christ and less of me is what we believers should pray for and sing about repeatedly. This is my heart's desire: less of my flesh and more of the power of the Spirit flowing in and through me!

Remember this: It starts with a word from God (revelation knowledge); then, this word must be accepted by faith. If we genuinely believe it is God moving in us by giving us His command, we will act on it! Action must always follow His instructions.

Take note: God is working through us to fulfill His heart's desire. Neh'en-ah.

28

Believe with the Heart and do It! - Part 3
Critical Factors in Visionary Leadership

"And they returned from spying out the land after forty days. Now they departed and came back to Moses and Aaron and all the congregation of the children of Israel in the Wilderness of Paran, at Kadesh; they brought back word to them and to all the congregation and showed them the fruit of the land. Then they told him and said: "We went to the land where you sent us. It truly flows with milk and honey, and this is its fruit. Nevertheless, the people who dwell in the land are strong; the cities are fortified and very large; moreover, we saw the descendants of Anak there. The Amalekites dwell in the land of the South; the Hittites, the Jebusites, and the Amorites dwell in the mountains; and the Canaanites dwell by the sea and along the banks of the Jordan. Then Caleb quieted the people before Moses and said, "Let us go up at once and take possession, for we are well able to overcome it." But the men who had gone up with him said, "We are not able to go up against the people, for they are stronger than we." And they gave the children of Israel a bad report of the land which they had spied out, saying, "The land through which we have gone as spies is a land that devours its inhabitants, and all the people whom we saw in it are men of great stature. There we saw the giants (the descendants of Anak came from the giants); and we were like grasshoppers in our own sight, and so we were in their sight." (Numbers 13:25-33)

The truth about God speaking into our lives is so we may understand His excellent plan; He then inspires us to go forth in His Name and receive the promise. Nothing encourages an individual more than when his heart is awakened with a new vision from heaven.

The children of Israel had received a great promise, and now the time had come for them to take possession of their land. There was only one small problem - they couldn't picture themselves entering.

You see, because they didn't trust the Lord's words during smaller challenges in the past, they would struggle with this big challenge now. It's the same way with us. The small test prepares us for the bigger ones!

In a bold and daring way, they challenged God to send spies to explore the promised land on their behalf. The spies were to go, evaluate the land, and then report their findings. This they did.

After forty days, the spies returned with a conclusion: We believe God is mighty, but did you really examine those giants? They seem unbeatable. So, they voted by majority (ten to two) not to take the land. This made God very angry!

How often do we miss out on wonderful chances to grow? Why do we let our hearts deceive us, even when they burn with conviction to move forward? What about our minds filled with prophetic visions of the promise, yet hindered by fear that some giant might crush us?

Today, thank God we are not like the ten spies who doubted and were afraid. You and I are not from the lineage of fear – **"For God has not given you the spirit of fear, but of love and power and a sound mind."** (2 Timothy 1:7)

We have been called to conquer every circumstance! Every test and trial only helps us grow and mature as our focus stays on the mountain peaks of prophetic promises. Just like Jesus our Lord, we have set our face like a flint and shaped our hearts toward our God-given destiny. We have everything we need to succeed!

When God speaks, His prophetic word performs three actions in us. Here they are:

1. Our mindset will change. Nothing is more convincing to our physical mind than God revealing His presence and pouring heavenly visions into our hearts. Once our mindset is captivated by a higher realm, our soul and body will follow.

2. Our souls will be revived. To be revived means to be made alive again or to come alive. Once our spirit imparts to our soul, every emotion will yearn for God's passionate heart and purpose.

3. Our body will be energized. Once our spirit and soul are awakened, our body — renewed with energy and anointing — will face everything in its way, including fears, doubts, failures, and uncertainties.

As I finish these words, take a moment to reflect on the last few notes in this series. God has already done everything necessary for you to succeed. If you are not growing, it might mean you're not living by faith. Everything God says must be followed for it to produce fruit.

If you are fruitless, it's not because God doesn't want to bless you. You might be fighting doubt and fear. It's time to examine your heart and bring it back to God's original design. Neh'enah.

29

No Wonder the Proud Ones Never Win!

"For you see your calling, brethren, that not many wise according to the flesh, not many mighty, not many noble, are called. But God has chosen the foolish things of the world to put to shame the wise, and God has chosen the weak things of the world to put to shame the things which are mighty; and the base things of the world and the things which are despised God has chosen, and the things which are not, to bring to nothing the things that are, that no flesh should glory in His presence." (1 Corinthians 1:27-29)

This week, I came across this part of God's Word during my quiet time and reflected on why God favors the humble and broken, showing His favor to them in astonishing ways.

Let me share a few things on this subject and explain why God releases this incredible favor upon those who truly grasp it.

The first truth we must accept is this: the Lord will not allow anything created to steal His glory; He won't permit any flesh to be glorified in His presence. A man can be driven by his abilities and talents to an unhealthy degree – it's possible! A man can be so proud and arrogant; by this, I mean to be so full of himself that God can't stand him. Listen to the words of James the Apostle: **"God resists the proud but gives grace to the humble"** (James 4:6). I didn't say it; James did!

What does the word resist mean? In its original Greek sense, it means to confront in battle, to stand against, or to oppose. How about that? The proud are disliked by those around them, and God Himself has opposed them. How would you like to be in a fight against God? Do you hear how foolish that sounds? Yet, too many try to outwit God. Is it any wonder the proud never win?

Now, let's explore another secret. Why does God feel so drawn to the humble and broken?

Humility and brokenness have always been the keys to God's favor. Those who embrace this lifestyle will never lack any good thing. How can anyone who seeks God first in all matters of life be left out in the cold by the Lord? It will never happen, for God is attracted to all those with the disposition to be a vessel for Him.

You see, God knows everything about the vessel. God knows every genuine intent of the heart. The humble have no interest in hiding themselves from their Maker. No wonder God is so drawn to this kind of heart; yes, those who are desperate for Him.

Leading with Brokenness!

The leadership of someone with a broken, humble heart is the most powerful weapon. God needs a platform to act; your heart and mine serve as that platform. If we humble ourselves, God will come and teach us about ourselves and our trade, and He will entrust us with the keys to govern effectively.

When the man or woman of God is passionate for God's glory to be revealed through them, and they seek humility with brokenness as their standard before the Lord, God will gently come and release His glory and power!

"For thou art a holy people unto the LORD thy God: the LORD thy God hath chosen thee to be a special people unto himself, above all people that are upon the face of the earth. The LORD did not set his love upon you, nor choose you, because ye were more in number than

any people; for ye were the fewest of all people..." (Deuteronomy 7:6, 7)

The Scripture in Deuteronomy shows that God did not choose Israel because they were a strong nation; He chose them because they were small and insignificant. God set His heart on them and loved them because of their humility. He will do the same for us.

We should never forget our place in God. He is first above all; He leads, and we follow! Neh'enah.

30

Unholy Hesitation!

"Then the eleven disciples went away into Galilee, to the mountain which Jesus had appointed for them. When they saw Him, they worshiped Him; but some doubted." (Matthew 28:16-17)

While in deep meditation this morning, I came across another passage in God's Word and felt the Spirit of God hover over me concerning this hidden truth. As I read and re-read this Scripture in Matthew 28, the Holy Spirit made me notice something that could significantly impact us negatively as faithful followers of Christ. So, let me share this vital truth as God revealed it to me.

Let's consider the context: Jesus had just risen from the dead and told His eleven disciples to meet Him in Galilee on the mountain. As they waited with anticipation to see what would happen, Jesus suddenly appeared. What happened in the minutes that followed in the lives of these disciples will teach us an important lesson about our understanding of Christ.

"When they saw Him..." I have never witnessed a resurrection, but if I ever had the chance, I can only imagine what that would do to my mind and heart. I know that, without a doubt, my faith would take a huge leap. Reflecting on the lives of these followers of Christ and their eyewitness account of His resurrection, one might think that after seeing Jesus resurrected in bodily form, the disciples would have all fallen face down and been overwhelmed with emotion over this miracle. Just imagine this!

Now, the Scripture does say that some **"worshiped Him."** But my critical observation makes me wonder why **"some doubted."** My immediate response would be, "How can you doubt? This is the risen Christ in flesh, blood, and living color. He was dead and now is alive! – Come on, people!"

In one way, I am shocked by their unbelief, but in another way, I am not surprised!

As I prayed and sought God about this matter, the Holy Spirit made it very clear to me: David, anything that comes from God must be received by faith. Only through the eyes and heart of faith can a man truly know God. It is the only way to see, understand, connect, be led, and receive anything from the Lord. James said it best in his epistle when he wrote, **"Only it must be in faith that he asks with no wavering (no hesitating, no doubting). The one who wavers (hesitates, doubts) is like the billowing surge out at sea that is blown hither and thither and tossed by the wind. For truly, let not such a person imagine that he will receive anything** [he asks for] **from the Lord,** [For being as he is] **a man of two minds (hesitating, dubious, irresolute),** [he is] **unstable and unreliable and uncertain about everything** [he thinks, feels, decides]." (James 1:6-8 AMP)

Here's my conclusion: If we hesitate to follow the Spirit of the Lord's guidance, we will end up with nothing. A double-minded person will never be able to see the great potential God has prepared for them. This unholy hesitation will hinder every blessing that could lead to a more extraordinary life for us who believe.

Two Types of Disciples

The disciples on the mountain in Galilee can be divided into two groups:
- (1) Those who saw Jesus and worshiped Him—these had eager hearts and quickly recognized the beauty of God in the resurrected Christ—and
- (2) the others, who tended to be hesitant and doubtful.

Doubting God might seem minor, but we'll quickly see that this mindset has a harmful impact. As a result, everything was put on hold for them. They became paralyzed by doubt and unbelief. Do you know anyone who is spiritually paralyzed? Maybe it's you! It's time to assess.

Perhaps it's just me, but I have never seen so many believers living with such fear and doubt; they seem to be overtaken by uncertainty, fear, and unbelief. Their lives appear to be constantly on pause, and nothing is ever done to fulfill God's purpose for them. Stagnation comes to mind.

Overcoming Disciples

I want to share a bit about how a disciple can overcome his fears, temptations, doubts, and so on.

Two things come to mind: Galatians 2:20, **"I have been crucified with Christ, and I no longer live, yet not I, but Christ lives in me."** This Scripture must become real in the servant's heart. If the servant of God doesn't die to self, he will continue battling uncertainties for the rest of his days.

Secondly, there is a need to actively practice fasting. Twenty-four hours without food equals one day of fasting. Commit to thirteen days of a small fast, plus spend an hour each morning in prayer; read a chapter of God's Word and apply it daily, and witness the power of God working in you – then be amazed!

I believe the time has come for us to trust God for what He has promised us. It's time to move forward with renewed passion and fresh zeal for the Lord and His church. It is time for God to lead us by His Spirit into our prophetic promises! Neh'enah.

31

It's Getting Very Windy Out There!

"Awake, O north wind, and come, O south! Blow upon my garden, that its spices may flow out." (Song of Solomon 4:16)

When we talk about God "moving," we can count on significant change happening! When God moves through our lives, things shift, and new things emerge.

Growth and change go hand in hand, and those who welcome change can transform their lives positively, OR they can be frozen by fear and doubt. The key lies in how we interpret the wind blowing upon us.

For some, strong winds have a negative effect. They feel attacked and overwhelmed by opposing forces. Others see the advantage of strong winds. They view it as a cleansing or removal of the old.

One of the biggest obstacles to any change is our mindset. People who train their minds and discipline themselves for challenges always learn the most valuable lessons and see the overall benefits even when facing opposition.

I have come to believe and know it to be true that there is no greater obstacle to our personal growth than our comfort zones. The familiar has always kept us safe and content until it loses its effectiveness.

It reminds me of the story of the Prophet Elijah when he was by the water brook. Listen: "**Then the word of the Lord came to him, saying, "Get away from here and turn eastward, and hide by the Brook Cherith, which flows into the Jordan. And it will be that you shall drink from** the brook, and I have commanded the ravens to feed you there." So, he went and did according to the word of the Lord, for he went and stayed by the Brook Cherith, which flows into the Jordan. The ravens brought him bread and meat in the morning and bread and meat in the evening; and he drank from the brook. And it happened after a while that the brook dried up, because there had been no rain in the land. Then the word of the Lord came to him, saying, "Arise, go to Zarephath, which belongs to Sidon, and dwell there. See, I have commanded a widow there to provide for you." (1 Kings 17:2-10)

Note that when the river dried up, God told Him to move. Along with the instruction to move, God told Elijah exactly where to go and how he would be provided for.

My dear friend and servant, can you see God extending your life to greater levels of faith? Can you see the Lord working in your life and lifting you to higher ground in Him? If you can't feel the Lord moving, then ask Him to reveal it to you. It is essential that you recognize His visitation in your life!

I believe that the Lord is moving once again, and He is guiding you and me toward a greater fullness—a place of more glory, deeper desire, and passion for His will to be fulfilled through our lives.

The biggest obstacle during Jesus' time was likely the religious groups of His day.

The Pharisees, Sadducees, and Scribes were part of the religious groups that held the "spiritual" authority over religion in Jerusalem. They followed the ancient teachings of the Law and the prophets. They had a clear goal: "Follow Moses!" Things had to be done through their authority, or else.

As far as they were concerned, anything different from what they had experienced, seen, or read was not of God. They were so religious that they couldn't see how they were missing the fullness of God.

Listen to Isaiah 35 – this chapter was recited repeatedly at their synagogue gatherings every Sabbath, every holiday, and so on. They never made the connection with the NOW!

They were suitable for following the Law and the prophets, but it was only half the revelation. The other half had come in the form of Jesus. **"And of His fullness, we have all received, and grace for grace. For the law was given through Moses, but grace and truth came through Jesus Christ."** (John 1:16-17)

The religious parties missed the great King's arrival and couldn't tolerate others seeing Him as King. Their jealousy eventually turned into hatred and murder.

Jesus performed many miracles on the Sabbath, which didn't "fly" too well with the religious leaders. They believed Jesus was breaking "the Law" of God by doing work on the Sabbath. Jesus told them that they didn't understand the Sabbath.

At one point, He told them that the Sabbath was made for man, not man for the Sabbath. And He said to them, "The Sabbath was made for man, and not man for the Sabbath. Therefore, the Son of Man is also Lord of the Sabbath." (Mark 2:27-28) In other words, man is not enslaved by a day, but that day can be used to glorify God.

Then came one of Jesus's most important statements to the Pharisees: **"Do not think that I came to destroy the Law or the Prophets. I did not come to destroy but to fulfill."** (Matthew 5:17)

As you can see, Jesus didn't break any laws or show disrespect to anyone; He came to fulfill what was missing. He came to complete what lacked.

He came to express the fullness of God!

"**And no one puts new wine into old wineskins; or else the new wine will burst the wineskins and be spilled, and the wineskins will be ruined. But new wine must be put into new wineskins, and both are preserved. And no one, having drunk old wine, immediately desires new; for he says, 'The old is better.'"** (Luke 5:37-39)

Jesus said that new wine must be placed in new wineskins. The old wineskins and containers would eventually break during fermentation, spilling all the new wine.

I believe Jesus was trying to show us that in the new move of God, we must renew our hearts and minds so we can CONTAIN the new thing God is doing. Our minds need to understand that God is leading us "into the land." Our hearts also need to expand and see that God is "demonstrating a bigger picture of Himself to us." This new move reveals another part of His nature.

It's true what Jesus says at the end of this verse: **"And no one, having drunk old wine, immediately desires new; for he says, "The old is better."** Isn't this the truth?

When we become comfortable with what we know, what we have seen and heard, or what doesn't require faith, we naturally conclude: "Why bother to learn something new or why walk on water when we can get inside a boat."

We must embrace God's new revelations because they are essential for our growth in Him. Whenever God starts to reveal Himself to us, it is to empower or guide us to go deeper into His plan. So let the winds blow upon your garden! Neh'enah.

32

Are You Aware of What God Is Doing in Your Life?

"Then the kingdom of heaven shall be likened to ten virgins who took their lamps and met the bridegroom. Now five of them were wise, and five were foolish. Those who were foolish took their lamps and took no oil with them, but the wise took oil in their vessels with their lamps. But while the bridegroom was delayed, they all slumbered and slept." (Matthew 25:1-5)

Many people read this part of Scripture and loudly declare that they see themselves as "wise." They say, "God forbid that I would be a fool."

It's interesting that Jesus used these verses to illustrate a point. In these Scripture passages, we find not just two groups of people but three. The first group is the prudent or wise virgins; the second group consists of the foolish virgins who didn't prepare with enough oil, and the third group includes us. We will decide how to respond to the situation at hand. Since both the wise and foolish groups fell asleep, what will my group do?

As I studied this part of Scripture, I realized that God desires His children to become wise in everyday life. Fools don't respect the Lord, and their reputation as failures often stays with them until the end. It's easy to spot a fool.

But as I pondered this, I heard the Lord say, "David, notice the wise and fools... what do they have in common? I looked at the Scripture, read it, and re-read it, and then it hit me - Ah! They both slumbered and fell asleep!

So, what is the main point of this passage? What was the Holy Spirit truly trying to instill in us?

For one, God is not impressed by my wisdom or how much I have achieved with it. And secondly, I don't think the Lord approves of a fool's lifestyle either. So, what is God's heart in this matter? God's heart must primarily concern the fact that whether we believe we are wise or foolish, both have the potential to fall asleep and slumber in life.

Many believers boast about their faith, Biblical knowledge, presentation skills, and personal charisma. I have heard some say, "Our church is doing this great thing or that great thing!" That is all well and good, but are they truly awake? God is not impressed with the works!

Here's the core issue: God is seeking those who are awake! Wisdom only matters if you're alert to the purpose it was meant for. Do you understand? If you're wise but asleep, it's the same as being dead—no difference.

In leadership, a leader must have a touch of God's presence burning brightly within. The person steering the ship must be alert every moment. They cannot sleep or slumber while on duty. You and I are no different. We are not only called to seek God's wisdom but also to stay awake in every area of our lives. Here are three things we must stay alert to and do everything possible to remain awake:

Always stay aware of God's Presence. If you have been born-again, the Spirit of the Lord lives in you. He will encourage you to be close to God. He will guide you to spend time in prayer and reading God's Word. Listen to what is inside your spirit. Please don't ignore it, or you will face serious consequences.

Always remain attentive to God's Will. There is a way that seems right to a person, but ultimately, it leads to death. This Proverb addresses a life controlled by the flesh. The flesh does not seek to follow God's will; if anything, it strives to divert us from fulfilling our purpose in God. When awakened, the Spirit of the Lord guides us into the mind and heart of God.

Always stay alert to God's Seasons. As you know, the seasons (summer, fall, winter, and spring) change around us at specific times, and so do the seasons of the Lord. We must remain alert to understand what season God is leading us into. You can't make something grow if you're in a winter season. You can't harvest in the spring — you see my point. We need to stay awake in God to recognize the seasons and the times.

As I close this devotion, we must realize that it is not what we have received from the Lord that sets us apart. What truly distinguishes us is walking out God's divine orders, and are we abiding under that given anointing today? Neh'enah.

33

A Portrait of the Slothful Servant!

"Lazy people are soon poor; hard workers get rich." (Proverbs 10:4 - NLT)

As I opened my eyes to the sound of my alarm, my mind started making decisions: should I get up now for prayer or sleep a little longer? As I debated, I heard the Spirit of God say, "The slothful end up in poverty!" I swear I could almost hear the Lord say this to me out loud. I quickly got up and committed my heart to seeking God's face.

During my prayer time, I started to ask about the words He had given me earlier, and as always, He revealed this incredible wisdom. Here is what the Lord taught me:

He told me that the lazy man consistently ends up in poverty. I know this from reading the Proverbs; the book of Proverbs is filled with instructions about laziness. Then the Lord said, "It is not the natural results of being lazy that I'm talking about. It's regarding the results in the spiritual realm. If a man doesn't spend time with Me, he will not know what to do, where to go, or even why he exists."

Also, the Lord taught me that without a dedicated "quiet time," His servants would lose their spiritual discernment. What is spiritual discernment? Discernment is the ability to judge wisely. Spiritual discernment involves perceiving without bias to gain spiritual guidance and insight.

A man who loses touch with God also loses his spiritual discernment, which can be tragic. Do you remember how all this started? Let me remind you: it all began with a decision to spend time with God or not.

Let us examine the consequences of a lazy life without prayer. The downward spiral starts by becoming poor in ...

Vision. Once our discernment is lost, we are left aimless and without direction. We don't know what steps to take. Our vision becomes unclear, and the most common outcome is that we fall into a ditch of despair. Nothing compares to being spiritually blind. Everything seems dark, and confusion constantly surrounds us.

Passion. The second thing we end up losing is our vitality and passion. We no longer look forward to the future; we are stuck in despair. Life is no longer enjoyable; we only have memories of what once was. Our passion drives our existence, but now it's gone. The best you and I can do is find a substitute. We will recreate with our hands what we have lost in our souls.

Prosperity. The last thing a man loses is his prosperity. The favor that once came with us has disappeared. All we hold onto are stories of how God used to speak to us, move within us, and bless us. The sadness in our hearts consumes us because we can sense that God is no longer working in or with us. Something has changed, and emptiness has become our portion.

Isn't this the portrait of a lazy man or woman? Why did this happen? Whose fault was it anyway? Can the lazy person, in all honesty, find someone to blame? Or was it his or her fault?

Friends, I have no doubt that it is the lazy man's fault, and the consequences show it.

Now, let's consider the blessing of someone who is diligent. A person who persists and desires God's glory in everything shows diligence. They are always eager for more of Jesus; they are not double-minded or hesitant. They hate sin and its effects and continually seek to live under the shadow of the Almighty (Psalm 91).

The results of such a person are compelling. For one, the diligent man possesses spiritual discernment because he spends time in God's presence, lost in adoration and willing to be changed by God's hand. This man has vision and passion. Prosperity (God's favor) follows him everywhere he goes. The Scripture says, **"The plans of the diligent lead surely to abundance..."** [Proverbs 21:5a – ESV]

There are lazy servants and diligent servants. The best part is that you and I can choose what we want to be! Neh'enah.

34

The Unlimitedness of God!

"After considerable time had elapsed, the Jews conspired to put Saul out of the way by slaying him, but [the knowledge of] their plot was made known to Saul. They were guarding the [city's] gates day and night to kill him, but his disciples took him at night and let him down through the [city's] wall, lowering him in a basket or hamper." (Acts 9:23-25 Amplified Version)

A few nights ago, the Lord visited me again with another prophetic dream, giving me a glimpse of His heart about teamwork. My dream wasn't very long, but I feel compelled by the Lord to share it with you, and I hope it will minister to you. My dream was as follows:

My dream took place outside my house. I was standing on my front porch, and a sidewalk extended from there to the street. The only unusual thing about this sidewalk was that it was about three steps high from the street. Up to that point, I had built steps two and three but still needed the first step. In other words, my staircase wasn't complete, and it included the bottom step. While I was outside observing, someone showed up at my house and immediately noticed my unfinished cement stairs. He asked me why I hadn't finished the bottom step. I replied, "I need to get a special molding to make my last step, and I don't think they have invented it yet." He quickly said, "Yes, they have been invented, and I know where you can find one." So, we found this molding to complete my stairs. We brought it home, worked on it, poured the cement, and finished the job—that was the end of the dream.

As I woke up, the Lord reminded me of the story above. The Apostle Paul was in serious danger, and there was no way he could escape the mob that wanted to kill him. They had been waiting for him day and night with the intention to kill him. When you might think that the devil has the victory, God will raise a standard against the enemy on your behalf. Listen to this: **"They were guarding the [city's] gates day and night to kill him, but his disciples took him at night and let him down through the [city's] wall, lowering him in a basket or hamper."**

Here's what I received from the Lord about my dream: God assured me that I should keep moving forward with His calling, vision, and the purpose He has placed in my heart. Some resources will come from within you; others will come through people you might not even know personally; and, of course, some resources will come supernaturally from the Lord. Don't limit yourself by thinking, "How will I get out of this?" or "Where am I going to get what I need?" or "I don't have the resources to do this or that!"

Just like in my dream, a man approached me and suggested I complete the final step to my set of stairs – I believe that God will come to you in different ways to open your anxious heart and fortify you with His wisdom.

When you live by worldly standards, you tend to train your mind to conform to natural ways of doing things. My experience with practicing worldly wisdom and standards has shown me that they can be limiting.

Now, when someone makes God their wisdom, everything changes! God will come and share His wisdom and understanding, and even bring those who know more than you to help empower you to accomplish the task.

All we need to know is that God has no limits; if we dare to live by God's standards, knowledge, and wisdom, the sky becomes our only limit. Neh'enah.

35

One Thing is Needed!

"Now it happened as they went that He entered a certain village, and a certain woman named Martha welcomed Him into her house. And she had a sister called Mary, who also sat at Jesus' feet and heard His word. But Martha was distracted with much serving, and she approached Him and said, "Lord, do You not care that my sister has left me to serve alone? Therefore, tell her to help me." And Jesus answered and said to her, "Martha, Martha, you are worried and troubled about many things. But one thing is needed, and Mary has chosen that good part, which will not be taken away from her." (Luke 10:38-42)

A few nights ago, the Holy Spirit gave me a prophetic dream that deeply spoke to my heart. I want to share this insight with you and enlighten you significantly. The only requirement is to open your heart to the Holy Spirit and be fully willing to receive whatever God may want to say to you personally.

My dream started when I led this large group of people that looked like a huge church congregation. A man walking beside me asked, "How did you manage to grow this ministry so quickly?" I told him, "I don't know – all I know is that God kept increasing the number of people incredibly fast. It began with just a few people, and now it has thousands. I don't understand how it all happened so fast." This concludes the first scene.

In my dream's second scene, I am driving a luxury foreign car. This car was expensive and very nice, and I had a parking spot at the church where I was the pastor. When I arrived, I noticed the key was melting and barely fit in the lock. I remember taking it out and wondering why it was melting. The car still started, but I wasn't sure for how long.

When I woke up, my heart felt troubled. I started to wonder what all of this meant, and over the week, I prayed and sought God about it. Here is what I believe God was telling me in this prophetic dream:

David, I need you to focus more on the key. In this dream, I prospered beyond measure, and the good life—both in the spiritual and natural realms—never felt so real. Yet, amidst this prosperity, I could hear God say that the key that makes all this work cannot melt. In other words, you can activate luxury in the spiritual or natural world with a key.

What is the key that makes everything work? It is the key to personal prayer and devotion to Jesus the King.

It is possible to become so absorbed in life's mundane, external things that we neglect the very thing that makes it all worthwhile—the purpose of God in our lives.

In the story mentioned above, Mary seemed eager to be at Jesus' feet, while Martha was more focused on activity and completing tasks. Jesus would ultimately be the judge of this situation. Here is what the King of the Universe said about this possible imbalance: **"Martha, Martha, you are worried and troubled about many things. But one thing is needed, and Mary has chosen that good part, which will not be taken away from her."**

Both are necessary: the time spent at Jesus' feet and the work with our hands to accomplish tasks. However, Jesus provided perspective for all who want to do it right. He said that Mary had chosen the good part! Therefore, Mary is praised for her desire to be at Jesus' feet rather than Martha's activity in the kitchen.

I have learned: Be at Jesus' feet in prayer and devotion and do whatever He shares with you!

As I conclude, remember, don't let the key melt. You will need it for everything you will ever accomplish. Neh'enah!

36

The Secret of Increase!

"And I will send hornets before you, which shall drive out the Hivite, the Canaanite, and the Hittite from before you. I will not drive them out from before you in one year, lest the land become desolate, and the beasts of the field become too numerous for you. Little by little, I will drive them out from before you until you have increased and inherited the land." (Exodus 23:28-30)

This powerful principle isn't very popular; like most life-changing and life-transforming principles, it usually gets pushed aside for something more "sparkly."

As I explained to someone the importance of consistently living out this principle I'm talking about, this person practically rolled his eyes and said, "Who has time to wait?!" Hearing this, it reminded me of how I was at his age; I would have responded just as quickly, "Who has time to wait?!"

The real fact is this: People who constantly try to do great things, venture into business or ministry, land a dream job, or attempt lifestyle changes rarely achieve their goals, and as a result, never reach their desired destination.

Why is this? Is the problem due to a lack of desire? Is the difficulty in overcoming certain bad habits because of no self-will? I see this differently. I believe that a person can have desires, dreams, ambitions, and self-will, but if they don't understand that progress comes from practicing the "little by little" principle daily, then they will never achieve their goals and dreams.

We all reach a certain age where we believe we can do everything through hard work. We have strength, stamina, vision, and passion, but often, we need more wisdom and understanding to accomplish anything.

People say, "He or she always has great ideas and starts them but never completes them!" Have you ever considered that you might be doing the same thing in your own life? Is anyone saying that about you? Would they be telling the truth?

Too often, immaturity overcomes us. We dream and act like little children but quickly give up and become impatient. We don't allocate enough time and effort into our long-term goals. We tend to get discouraged and end up back at the drawing board. My friends, this must change if we are to succeed.

The *"Little by Little Principle"* means a lot to me personally. This principle says,

I will walk with you if you walk with me. If you trust me, I will help make all your dreams and visions come true. I might not give you everything you want immediately, but I will eventually deliver it. While you patiently wait for me to do my part, you will be shaped by the delays. Soon, you'll see the results of your efforts as you keep sowing into them. Once your dream becomes reality, I will celebrate with you, and you'll be glad I was there with you every step of the way. Who am I? I am the *"Little by Little Principle."* I am the one who makes it happen for you if you trust me.

As I write, I realize we live in a fast-paced world. Nothing can be too quick for us. Microwaves, computers, smartphones, cars, bank tellers, ATMs, supermarket cashiers, customer service – yes, we expect everyone to be quick. The only issue is that things of value don't come quickly.

Valuable things are cultivated gradually until they appear. Diamonds, pearls, gold, and oil are all highly valuable. The only thing about these elements is that you don't find them on the surface. You must dig repeatedly until they are discovered.

In most cases, one must spend a fortune before discovering a diamond or a nugget of gold. When the seeker finally finds a diamond, nugget of gold, or strikes oil, they realize its true value and become personally valuable because of the lessons learned during the search for their treasure.

Little by little, we dig every day until one day—bang! The *"little by little principle"* does its perfect work, and it rewards us handsomely! Neh'enah.

37

Are You Too Busy to Worship?

"Then Pharaoh called to Moses and said, "Go, serve the LORD; only let your flocks and your herds be kept back. Let your little ones also go with you." But Moses said, "You must also give us sacrifices and burnt offerings, that we may sacrifice to the LORD our God. Our livestock also shall go with us; not a hoof shall be left behind. For we must take some of them to serve the LORD our God, and even we do not know with what we must serve the LORD until we arrive there." (Exodus 10:24-26)

The most powerful weapon behind everything we do isn't how many people we know, how many contacts we might have, or how many "strings" we can pull. It's not our charisma, how diplomatic we can be, or even our social status.

I believe the most influential people on earth are those who know God deeply and personally. These individuals are the ones who keep this world functioning; their personal understanding of God's holiness is what genuinely brings order to our world.

I also believe that the most powerful weapon for anyone wanting to advance God's kingdom through their ministry or vocation is a heart of true worship!

True worship is a response to God, an act or expression of kindness for all He has done. It is a private acknowledgment in our inner selves of His greatness and awesomeness, allowing Him to immerse us in His glorious presence. Keep in mind, this is how His glory is reflected in our countenance.

The Devil Will Try to Get You to Compromise!

Now, let's revisit the Scripture in Exodus and I will outline some points to help clarify what I believe God is saying.

First, please note that Pharaoh represents a symbol or type of the enemy of our souls.

Pharaoh represents the world, our flesh (carnal nature), or Satan himself. The enemy is always planning and organizing continuous efforts to keep us from true worship, which connects our spirit with God's Spirit. Also, true worship is not just songs, prayers, or religious clichés. True worship goes much deeper than that! It's about the heart of man engaging with God's heart.

Secondly, genuine worship will always come with a cost.

True worship is costly and will require everything from us. We must be willing to surrender all our emotions, plans, ambitions, dreams, and more so we can honor Him with a fully surrendered heart. This is not easy—especially when we're caught up with self and its desires.

In your prayer, say, "Jesus, I come before you to lay everything at your feet. As I give you everything, only give me back what you want me to have! My heart is Yours and only Yours!" Amen.

So, the key to entering true worship involves letting go of all our ideas or idols – until our hearts become neutral. Once we reach this point, we can worship in spirit and truth.

Interestingly, Pharaoh didn't mind them (Moses and God's people) going into the desert to worship; he just made sure that no animals were taken for sacrifices. What would they offer Jehovah God?

My friends, if you haven't realized this yet, it's time we did; listen, the devil isn't stupid! He will try to get you to rush out the door into your busy schedule without offering a sacrifice of worship. The rule of true worship is that if nothing dies, it probably means there was no sacrifice; therefore, there is no true worship! If we don't die to our fleshly desires and offer ourselves to the living God in worship every day, then we are defaulting to offering worship to ourselves!

In closing, remind yourself every morning before leaving your house and venturing out to pursue your great dream – don't leave without spending quality time in true worship.

There's nothing quite like having your face transformed and your eyes shining with the beautiful light of God within you; yes, all of this is made possible through genuine worship. Neh'enah.

38

Wake Up! Class Is In Session.

"And Peter answered him and said, Lord, if it be thou, bid me come unto thee on the water. And he said, Come. And when Peter was come down out of the ship, he walked on the water, to go to Jesus. But when he saw the wind boisterous, he was afraid; and beginning to sink, he cried, saying, Lord, save me." (Matthew 14:28-30)

"And a great windstorm arose, and the waves beat into the boat, so that it was already filling. But He was in the stern, asleep on a pillow. And they awoke Him and said to Him, "Teacher, do You not care that we are perishing? Then He arose and rebuked the wind, and said to the sea, "Peace, be still!" And the wind ceased and there was a great calm. But He said to them, "Why are you so fearful? How is it that you have no faith?" And they feared exceedingly, and said to one another, "Who can this be, that even the wind and the sea obey Him!" (Mark 4:37-41)

Note the word 'wind' in the two passages I mentioned earlier. In Matthew, the wind was boisterous; in Mark, it was a windstorm. In both cases, the winds appeared to be God's way or means of testing spiritual depth and maturity.

Things haven't changed much for the aspiring leader eager to deepen his mission, vocation, or ministry. It seems that the factor prompting someone to honestly assess their life is beyond control – in this case, it was the wind.

For those who have never learned from trials but have always zigzagged through life, avoiding potential winds of adversity can be devastating.

Nothing builds our character more than a tough windstorm in life or a situation entirely out of our control. God tests us to the core by allowing circumstances that push us to our wits' end.

Remember: when life's winds start to blow, don't be afraid. Know that it's time to grow a little deeper in Him. Here are a few reasons why we shouldn't fear the winds of life.

1. He created the winds. If you believe in God and have been born again, then you will also know that God created the heavens, the earth, and everything in it. If you belong to God, He is your Heavenly Father and will always have His eye on you. You can rest in His everlasting arms. Whatever you are facing now, the Father knows about it and will com fort you in every way.

2. The winds are under His control. Another important point is that the seas and winds obey Him. All of creation is subject to His authority. Nothing will touch you unless God permits it. Even the devil is under God's authority. So, if you're facing a trial right now, remember that God is allowing it! Learn from it.

3. The winds are temporary – they will pass. Every challenge you and I face has a time limit. You will only be tested until you learn the valuable lesson behind it. The sooner you learn, the sooner the test ends. Winds are just temporary wake-up calls reminding us that spiritual education is happening.

4. The winds will awaken the Jesus in you! What will you do when the wind is destroying your boat (life) and your boat is sinking miserably? Who are you going to call upon? The United States Coast Guard? The Navy? Do what the disciples did: they woke Jesus up! Once Jesus was awakened, the winds ran for cover! Wake up the Jesus that might be sleeping in your own heart. Trust me, He will know exactly what to do with the wind in your life!

5. The winds are God's way of teaching us and helping us grow. Some life lessons are more valuable than a million dollars. What we learn through much hardship and testing will serve us well in the future. It will benefit you, and those who follow your leadership will be deeply influenced. The results of your perseverance will be like sweet music to someone navigating their own stormy seas.

May the Lord continue to guide and lead us through our exciting journey. The wind is not as bad as it seems; it is a blessing in disguise. As Bob Dylan eloquently wrote, "The answer, my friend, is blowing in the wind." [Genesis 8:1; Psalm 18:10; Psalm 107:23-30] Neh'enah.

39

Don't Get "Wowed" by What You See!

"Therefore, whoever hears these sayings of Mine, and does them, I will liken him to a wise man who built his house on the rock: and the rain descended, the floods came, and the winds blew and beat on that house; and it did not fall, for it was founded on the rock. "But everyone who hears these sayings of Mine, and does not do them, will be like a foolish man who built his house on the sand: and the rain descended, the floods came, and the winds blew and beat on that house, and it fell. And great was its fall." (Matthew 7:24-27)

If you don't get "wowed" by what you see – you won't get "discouraged" by what you don't see.

Just like a house relies on its foundation for durability, our lives also depend on a solid foundation. The foundation of any bridge, house, building, or life will determine its outcome.

Of course, since a foundation is never visible, people tend to overlook it. How can you assign value to something that isn't even seen? That's exactly my point! All too often, we fall in love with something based on its external appearance and are so amazed by its outward beauty that we rarely question what's supporting that building, business, or person's life.

Typically, people applaud a man's accomplishments. When the man falls into some embarrassing sin, corruption, crime, or faces the collapse of a business or ministry, everyone is shocked by it. People quickly ask, "Why?" or "How could this happen?" I'm sure you have heard these comments. They sound like this: "How could they have done that to themselves? They had so many friends!" "How could they have stolen all that money? Did they not know they would get caught?" "How about the one who broke into a store to steal, being that he was a multi-millionaire?"

All these things happen daily, and again, where did the person go wrong? It all comes down to the depth of the foundation, or no foundation at all.

Let me share with you what has helped me "keep the flow" in my life and ministry for almost 30 years. As I said earlier, a foundation determines the durability of whatever you are building. The deeper, stronger, and more solid your foundation is, the longer-lasting your results will be.

My personal foundation is built on three pillars of truth. I have held onto these dearly, and they have served me well. I want to pass them on to you as you become a man or woman of value who aims to create long-lasting results.

When asked why I don't have a care in the world, as if I knew God and believed that everything would be okay, I will always answer and say, "I feel like this because... I know God, I know who I am, and I know where I am going."

First Pillar: "I know God! In my relationship with God, I make it a point to know Him intimately. I don't care much about external religion or what people say about Christianity. All I know is that I know God. I love God and will forever walk with Him. In my loving relationship with Jesus Christ, I can be open and honest with Him; He does the same with me. Knowing God is all about intimacy. When you reach the point of touching His heart, what other thing can you possibly need or want in life?"

Second Pillar: I know who I am! My confidence comes from my relationship with God. I know who I am because He has revealed it to me. I am unique, wonderfully made, created in His image, and given the privilege to live for Him. It doesn't matter what others think of me; my worth is from God. He is the only audience I aim to please. All of this is an internal work of God deep within me. All life originates from God. When your foundation is built on God's perspective on living, life can be incredible!

Third Pillar: I Know Where I'm Going! When you realize that everything you've become comes from God, your heart naturally fills with gratitude. All the gifts, talents, abilities, and opportunities that come your way serve as a platform to show how great God is. Your life's work isn't mainly about you, but about Him! Reaching a point of convergence in your personal life means revealing God's glory to everyone around you! What a wonderful time to be alive!

Please understand that it is not what you do, but who you are that makes life sweet and unique. Yes, how can you lose when your life comes from God? The Scripture says in John 1:4, **"In Him was life, and the life was the light of men."**

Can your life be full of joy, peace, faith, and expectation? Absolutely! All it takes is building a solid foundation and establishing your life. Learn that life is about taking your time to make it happen. Everything else is just icing on the cake. Neh'enah.

40

God Will Bring Us Full Circle!

"Now the word of the LORD came to Jonah, the son of Amittai, saying, "Arise, go to Nineveh, that great city, and cry out against it; for their wickedness has come up before Me." But Jonah arose to flee to Tarshish from the presence of the LORD. He went down to Joppa and found a ship going to Tarshish, so he paid the fare and went down into it to go with them to Tarshish from the presence of the LORD. But the LORD sent out a great wind on the sea, and there was a mighty tempest on the sea so that the ship was about to be broken up. Then the mariners were afraid; and every man cried out to his god, and threw the cargo that was in the ship into the sea, to lighten the load. But Jonah had gone down into the lowest parts of the ship, had lain down, and was fast asleep." (Jonah 1:1-5)

During my prayer time this week, the Holy Spirit reminded me of a fundamental principle I heard from a dear man of God several years ago.

While going through a period of change in his life, he said he chose a path that led him away from God's perfect will into His acceptable will. For those who are closest to Jesus, you know there is a big difference between these two roads.

He mentioned that in 1972, God challenged him to choose a specific path, and he chose the one he felt was better for himself. As a result, this decision turned out to be his own, not God's.

I heard this man speak this word back in 2010. Thirty-eight years had passed when the Lord finally caught up with him and told him, "You have been going the wrong way. In 1972, I told you to go this way, but you ran the opposite direction. You have spent thirty-eight years doing your own thing – it's time for you to do my thing!"

There is a character in the Bible named Jonah. Who hasn't heard about Jonah and his rebellious heart toward God? Jonah was a man of God who trusted in God completely until God asked him to do something he didn't want to do.

God wanted to save the city of Nineveh and needed a man to go and tell them to repent, so God chose Jonah. The only problem was that Jonah hated the Ninevites with a passion. He believed they deserved to be judged by God because they were evil. In his zeal, Jonah said, "I'm not going! Get someone else to do it!" and "[he] **arose to flee to Tarshish from the presence of the LORD."**

That is a bold move, if you ask me. He turned away from the presence of the Lord, or at least he thought he did. God had prepared several ways to bring this man of God back to his senses - this shows the mercy of God. God prepared a boat, a storm, and a big fish to accomplish the task.

The part that intrigued me the most was this verse: **"But Jonah had gone down into the lowest parts of the ship, had lain down, and was fast asleep."** When God calls us to do something for Him, He won't stop until He gets His way. Jonah went to lie down at the lowest part of the boat and fell asleep.

Have you ever tried to pretend that God didn't speak, unveil, or command a task to you? Many of us have followed this pattern before and, like Jonah, have been trapped inside our own prison cell.

Dear friends, we can't fall asleep or pretend to be sleeping when God needs us to fulfill a purpose.

Way too often, believers pretend to be asleep and act as if God hasn't given them a purpose, avoiding the responsibilities they have. We can miss God's perfect plan for our lives despite facing fear, doubt, or unbelief. Even worse, this act of disobedience can carry generational consequences!

Here's what I've learned: God will always achieve His purpose. Even if He had to use a storm and a fish to guide Jonah into obedience, He would also use every situation to bring us into alignment.

Remember, the ignorant keep retaking the test, but the prudent and wise grasp the seriousness of God's perfect will. Neh'enah.

41

When Good Things Start to Come in Bunches Your Way!

"[Joseph] took and sent helpings to them from before him, but Benjamin's portion was five times as much as any of theirs. And they drank freely and were merry with him." (Genesis 43:34)

While meditating upon this portion of Scripture, I was so moved by God's Holy Spirit to notice how Benjamin (Joseph's younger brother) was blessed five times more than his ten older brothers. I mean, I get it. Joseph had not seen his younger brother in over twenty years. But is this why he poured on him five times more than the rest? It truly made me wonder.

I began seeking God for revelation on this, and here's what the Holy Spirit began to show me. He told me, "David, Benjamin wasn't receiving royal treatment because he was the youngest; he was receiving it because of my favor over his life!" In this story, Joseph is a type of God, and Benjamin represents one of us— the church— who walk with God.

The Lord kept talking to me about the word favor. What is favor? Who receives favor? Why does someone get favor? How can a person keep living in favor? Let me try to answer these questions for you, as I feel the Spirit of the Lord on me to teach and reveal this one truth.

What is favor? Merriam-Webster's Dictionary defines *favor* as (1) friendly regard shown toward another, especially by a superior, (2) approving consideration or attention. Another clear definition is gracious kindness. It also refers to a special privilege, right granted, or conceded.

When someone walks under the covering of God's favor, it's natural to notice they have a confident demeanor. They know that God's hand (favor) is upon them. They aren't trying to be cocky, arrogant, or act proud in a negative way. No, these servants of the Lord have a deep understanding that God is for them! It has been revealed that God approves of them—this is a powerful confidence booster!

Who receives favor? Favor is granted to those who have come under the guidance and authority of the Lord. God looks at the heart. When God chooses to favor someone, it is because their hearts are soft, tender, pliable, and deeply submissive to Him. Additionally, someone who has come under the blood of Jesus and washed away their sins will find favor in God's eyes. When an individual aligns himself with God's purpose, favor will always follow them.

Why does someone find favor in God's eyes? An individual receives God's favor because God desires to show Himself to them in a meaningful way. When a servant visits a king, he must always bring a gift. It is the protocol in a monarchy. When the king sees the gift, he is immediately compelled to go above and beyond; he wants to demonstrate his great kindness, power, and provision. Similarly, as God's servants, we come to Him with a gift of worship and a humble heart. Imagine how God is prompted to show His great kindness and favor to us. Therefore, I firmly believe that offering worship and a contrite heart is essential to gaining favor with God.

How does one maintain this favorable lifestyle? To keep yourself under the flow of God's favor, all you need to do is acknowledge that He reigns over all the earth, in your heart, and over everything you now have and hope to have! Always give King Jesus the preeminence in everything, and His favor will never leave your life!

In closing, I believe that when a man seeks the heart of God, meaning His interests, the Lord will greatly favor such a servant. In short, if we favor Him, He will favor us! Neh'enah.

42

Beware of the Spirit of Slumber!

"Then Jesus came with them to a place called Gethsemane and said to the disciples, "Sit here while I go and pray over there." And He took with Him Peter and the two sons of Zebedee, and He began to be sorrowful and deeply distressed. Then He said to them, "My soul is exceedingly sorrowful, even to death. Stay here and watch with Me." He went a little farther and fell on His face, and prayed, saying, "O My Father, if it is possible, let this cup pass from Me; nevertheless, not as I will, but as You will." Then He came to the disciples and found them sleeping, and said to Peter, "What! Could you not watch with Me one hour? Watch and pray, lest you enter temptation. The spirit indeed is willing, but the flesh is weak." (Matthew 26:36-41)

With everything you've got, and I mean with all your strength, don't fall asleep! You might miss the most important experience of your life yet!

What is it about people who are always missing out on life's most important opportunities? Is it that they don't care about progressing in life? Is it a mental issue? Or is it a mindset that says, "You don't need anything meaningful in life; you are perfectly fine with how your life is going!" I don't know about you, but this attitude in a person irritates me! I mean, how can someone live such a negligent, meaningless lifestyle?

The Disciples Didn't Get It!

The disciples of Christ didn't fully understand who Jesus was or what He was trying to achieve during His thirty-three years on earth. They weren't convinced by His teachings about the coming kingdom of God and how they would influence society through godly principles and actions. So, when Jesus went to Gethsemane to pour out His heart to the heavenly Father, they thought it was just another prayer meeting.

The disciples (mainly John, James, and Peter) could not perceive the seasons of God or even understand why Jesus called them three out of the group of twelve. The Lord was about to make the most important decision that would ultimately affect Him, His followers, and the world for generations to come.

When the Lord left them to pray alone, the Scripture says He went further to pray to the Father. After spending some excruciating and heart-wrenching time in prayer, Jesus returned to the disciples, who had fallen asleep.

How would you like this group of supporters by your side during your most important moment of need?

Asleep At the Watch of the Lord!

I want to bring your attention to one thing—sleeping when you should be watching.

Let me try to break this down for you:

When I talk about sleeping, I'm not referring to sleeping at night. My concern is with a spirit of slumber that comes over your life when nothing seems to be happening; you know, when everything appears to be at a standstill, and there's no movement in you or around you.

These are spiritual times when a person is walking without the awareness of God. Have you ever experienced this?

Here are a few tips on how to wake up from the slumber:

  1. *Prayer.* Spend quality time in God's presence and invite Him to move

within you by allowing Him to come in and speak to your heart.

2. *Spirit of Submission and Brokenness.* Attitude is everything in the secret closet of prayer. Remember that you are not in charge of your life - He is!

3. *Read a chapter of the Bible, preferably from the New Testament.* Let God speak to you through His Word. Whenever you read anything in the Bible, God is talking directly to you.

4. *Journal or write down your findings.* Whatever God speaks to you in your reading, write it down and date it. If you like, you can add a title to your entry so you can go back and pray it again later.

Beware!

Be careful not to fall asleep and miss what God is doing in your life. Falling asleep can be harmful. It can disorient your life, family, ministry, and career.

Remember this: We only become sleepy when our hearts and minds are not engaged in what God is saying or doing. Tuning ourselves to the Lord's frequency requires effort; that's why we must always stay alert in His presence!

Let us keep our soul alive in God, focus our mind on His will, and ignite our spirit with His vision! Neh'enah.

43

The Diligent!

"He becomes poor who works with a slack and idle hand, but the hand of the diligent makes rich." (Proverbs 10:4 -*Amplified Version*)

In the book of Proverbs, written mainly by Solomon, the son of David, you will find the world's greatest manual, curriculum, and/or textbook on God's wisdom. One of the beautiful aspects of the Book of Proverbs is that it's written with a lot of cause and effect.

If the reader or student is determined to apply these godly principles of wisdom in their own daily life, it could potentially transform their entire life, leading to long-lasting effects that will, in turn, influence future generations.

As I studied chapter 10 of Proverbs, I came across this verse: "**...the diligent makes rich.**" I spent some time in prayer and reflection on this, and as I allowed the Lord to teach me, I heard the Spirit of the Lord say to me, *David, I will always make a way for the diligent.*

So, in the spirit of a learner, I want to share my findings on this word with you. If you approach it as initially intended, I'm sure it will serve as a key that opens doors for you like never before.

The Word Diligent Defined.

The word *diligent* means interestedly and persistently attentive; steady and earnest in applying oneself to a subject or pursuit; assiduous; and/or diligent. It describes a person who wholeheartedly dedicates their passion and effort to the pursuit of a worthy ideal.

The Word of God says that a diligent person will become rich. You don't have to be a rocket scientist to figure this out. Those who pay attention to a cause and work hard on it will never go without.

Henry Wadsworth Longfellow once said, *The heights by great men reached and kept were not attained by sudden flight, but they, while their companions slept, were toiling upward in the night.*

So, what does it really mean to be diligent in the world we live in today?

Here is what I believe the Lord is revealing to those who have an ear to hear: I believe diligent people are those who have seen the Promised Land (their personal vision) and work extra hours to reach it. Their ability to envision the future shapes their life philosophy and intentional way of living.

The diligent people wake up earlier than most and dedicate their early morning hours to what is valuable. For some, it is meditation, prayer, and worship. They clearly understand that vitality comes from within, not from the outside world.

Diligent people also arrive at work earlier than most. They work harder and longer. They usually turn on the lights before anyone else arrives and turn them off after everyone has gone home.

Yes, these hardworking, unknown individuals study harder, sacrifice more, give more, and go to great lengths to improve themselves. These are the people who will start movements and businesses, change nations, influence society, and help others come out of their shadows. Did I mention that they will also stand before kings? **"Do you see a man diligent and skillful in his business? He will stand before kings; he will not stand before obscure men."** (Proverbs 22:29)

Diligent people will always receive the best portion in life. You see, God seems to reward those who believe in and practice biblical principles. These individuals are not interested in keeping up with others; no sir, they are racing against themselves and looking at the face of Christ for the perfect pattern to follow!

I believe this is the place where they distance themselves from those enamored with the idea of making a name for themselves rather than glorifying God.

My message to you today is: *With everything you have, become diligent!* Neh'enah.

44

The Jacob in All of Us!

"Then Jacob was left alone, and a Man wrestled with him until the breaking of day." (Genesis 32:24)

Here's a story about a man God chose to help create a mighty nation called Israel. The end of his life is a great legacy for all humanity, but the start of Jacob's story wasn't very impressive. It reminds me how most of our lives are too. Life's circumstances have shaped us all to some extent.

Jacob was a young man who had a twin brother named Esau. Now, Esau was probably not as clever as Jacob and would often cheat him out of things. For example, Jacob stole Esau's birthright when they were young. On another occasion, Jacob had his father Isaac pray over him, pretending to be the firstborn, and the father gave the firstborn's blessing to him. Jacob was dishonest and took advantage of his father's poor eyesight. When I recount this story, it brings a lot to my mind.

It shows me that, as a human being, I am so much like Jacob. And honestly, without trying to be too judgmental, we all have a lot of Jacob in us.

Jacob represents the essence of selfishness. He embodies the selfish nature of our old self, reflecting all we are without Christ living in our hearts—a life lacking God's Spirit and life. We all need to be transformed out of this terrible evil that remains hidden or dormant in the old nature of Adam.

So, what can God do to bring about this much-needed change in us?

Let me share with you what I believe are some of God's tools for growing our lives and strengthening our character.

1. God allows tests and trials to come our way. We all are tested in our character. Sometimes, our trials are many and painful. When you face multiple trials in your life, always remember that God is not trying to harm you. He is transforming you into His image.

2. The Testing of Our Patience. Impatience shows immaturity. Impatient people often ignore others without thought. Have you ever noticed how you tend to break rules when you're in a hurry, something you'd usually avoid if you remained calm and composed? Clearly, God wants to shape our lives from the inside out.

3. Our Daily Decisions & Choices: Taking Shortcuts. Taking shortcuts will eventually catch up with us. Shortcuts in life tend to cheat us out of genuine character development. Character development is truly the foundation for a great future. Without a solid foundation, we can't build a meaningful future. Taking the "long way" leaves us with a sense of accomplishment and strengthens our character. When we decide to take the shortcut to anything, we only hurt ourselves and deny ourselves the valuable lesson of perseverance in our growth.

Jacob eventually arrived at the place where he met God (an Angel) and faced someone more intelligent, larger, and stronger than he was. It was at this moment in his life that Jacob was transformed.

Unless we have a close encounter with God Himself, our lives will keep falling into the same patterns. Remember, our minds and hearts must change for transformation to happen. If this doesn't occur, nothing will shift.

If you ever wonder why the same things keep happening to you repeatedly, wonder no more! My pastor used to say that if you want to keep getting what you're getting, then keep doing what you're doing! The need for a change from the inside out is the heartfelt cry of the Spirit that yearns jealously within us.

So, in closing, if you are facing difficult situations right now, know that God has set you apart for transformation. Neh'enah.

45

Flourish Where You Presently Are!

"There was a famine in the land, besides the first famine that was in the days of Abraham. And Isaac went to Abimelech king of the Philistines, in Gerar. Then the LORD appeared to him and said: "Do not go down to Egypt; live in the land of which I shall tell you. Dwell in this land, and I will be with you and bless you; for to you and your descendants I give all these lands, and I will perform the oath which I swore to Abraham your father. And I will make your descendants multiply as the stars of heaven; I will give to your descendants all these lands; and in your seed, all the nations of the earth shall be blessed; because Abraham obeyed My voice and kept My charge, My commandments, My statutes, and My laws." (Genesis 26:1-5)

The story of Isaac reminds me of many experiences I've had in my walk with the Lord. There were times when pressure heavily influenced my decisions, and honestly, I didn't always make the right choices. Have you ever been in this place in your own life?

I have always believed that pressure is one of God's greatest tools for shaping our character and helping us grow into the kind of man or woman He desires. Most influential people who have made a significant impact on society are those who have faced a lot of pressure.

Here's something worth knowing and noting: Pressure can be your greatest ally or your worst foe.

Whenever I encounter someone who constantly complains about how tough life is at work or in some situation, my first instinct is that they are being prepared for something bigger!

No one likes pain, struggle, and confusion in their personal lives. Most people don't see the value in adversity, but it's incredibly beneficial. So, the temptation is always to do everything right and take all precautions to ensure things turn out well; however, pressure tends to find us. Have you experienced this to be true?

Webster's Dictionary defines *pressure* as 1) The act of pressing, or the condition of being pressed; compression; a squeezing; a crushing; as a pressure of the hand 2) A contrasting force or impulse of any kind; as the pressure of poverty; the pressure of taxes; the pressure of motives on the mind; the pressure of civilization 3) Affliction; distress; grievance 4) Urgency 5) Impression; stamp; character impressed.

As you meditate on these definitions of pressure, you will realize that pressure plays a crucial role in shaping us toward God's intended image. Without pressure, we will never be moved to the right place or be challenged deeply enough to test our spiritual strength, newfound wisdom in God's word, and our God-given convictions and principles. So, in short, pressure is a perfect thing!

Let us take a quick look at the story above. Isaac is facing pressure; a famine has come, and he must make a choice. Isaac says, "Times are hard, and I must do something before we lose everything! I think I'll talk to Abimelech, the king of the Philistines, and see what advice I can get from him. Or maybe I should head down to Egypt and put all of God's plans on hold until this famine passes. After all, God won't get mad at me; He understands - it's a famine, for crying out loud! Why make it hard on myself, my family, and my business? Let me go and take refuge in Egypt for a bit."

Listen to the Lord, who knows our hearts:

Then the LORD appeared to him and said: "Do not go down to Egypt; live in the land of which I shall tell you. Dwell in this land, and I will be with you and bless you; for to you and your descendants I give all

these lands, and I will perform the oath which I swore to Abraham your father. And I will make your descendants multiply as the stars of heaven; I will give to your descendants all these lands; and in your seed, all the nations of the earth shall be blessed; because Abraham obeyed My voice and kept My charge, My commandments, My statutes, and My laws."

God told Isaac, "DO NOT go down to Egypt; live in the land of which I shall tell you. Dwell in this land, and I will be with you and bless you..." These words from God to Isaac were words of destiny. God said to Isaac, "I want to do something profound in your life, Isaac. Please don't ruin my plans! I've been waiting for you to face this famine. Don't take the shortcut; don't take the easy way out. Let this famine become your greatest opportunity! Plus, I will be with you and bless you. I can take care of you even during difficult circumstances. I can make things happen, even if your natural eyes see the opposite. I am Jehovah Jireh, your Provider!

My dear friends, we need to learn to thrive where God has placed us. It has never been about the famine, the hardship, the tough conditions, the countless temptations, the draining financial situation, or the wild emotional roller-coaster rides. It has all been about building and developing our character. It has all been for our benefit! Isaac eventually understood that. Neh'enah.

46

Why Am I Being Stirred Within?

"Now Isaac pleaded with the LORD for his wife because she was barren; and the LORD granted his plea, and Rebekah his wife conceived. But the children struggled together within her; and she said, "If all is well, why am I like this?" So, she went to inquire of the LORD. And the LORD said to her: "Two nations are in your womb, two peoples shall be separated from your body; one people shall be stronger than the other, and the older shall serve the younger." (Genesis 25:21-23a)

Have you ever felt a subtle confusion or deep unrest inside? Despite everything appearing normal on the outside, there is a lot of chaos within. Externally, everything seems to be in its right place. The sun still rises in the East and sets in the West, yet your heart feels wild, and your mind keeps spinning without providing an answer to your chaotic state. What is this? What do you call moments like these?

As I meditated on this part of Scripture, I learned that Rebecca was pregnant, and everything seemed to be going smoothly with the pregnancy. So, what made her ask, "If all is well, why am I like this?" It's clear from the text that, on the outside, everything looked fine, but inside, an emotion was awakening. It's characteristic of the Lord to lead His people this way.

I have noticed, at least in my own life, that when my heart is strangely stirred, it is usually because something in my life or sphere of influence needs attention. In that same awkward feeling or stirring, God may say to me, "David, something is out of alignment. Take the time to fix it." God is gracious and merciful; He will show us the issue.

You see, God rules the hearts of men, and when God wants or desires something to happen, all He has to do is stir our hearts emotionally into action. He causes us to love or hate something. He causes us to rise or sit. He causes us to walk or run after a thing. It is God's way of making things happen in our world.

This emotion Rebecca was experiencing was significant. She knew something was weighing on the Lord's heart. She needed an honest answer, and no one else could provide it. So, she did what every wise follower of God would do, "**...she went to inquire of the Lord.**"

God revealed to Rebecca what she was feeling. God made her know that there were twins in her womb. **"Two nations are in your womb..."** and there was a tremendous conflict coming. No wonder she was troubled and in much distress during her pregnancy.

My friends, God leads us by His Spirit first and foremost. Either we are at perfect peace or in distress over some matter. We always know God's will for our lives by the peace we feel in our hearts. Our peace is our gauge. Don't ever forget this.

We must make leadership decisions in this world—whether in work, family, ministry, school, or even politics. Our lives might seem okay from where we stand, but we should listen for the stirring of God's heart. God may very well be saying something profound and subtle to our hearts.

Before forming any conclusions about how you feel, seek God first and allow Him to reveal the "why' behind your emotions. God's choice will always bring peace to our hearts. A selfish decision, on the other hand, will often lead to turmoil and distress in our spirit. Neh'enah.

47

Why God Wants to Take You for a Ride!

"On the same day, when evening had come, He said to them, "Let us cross over to the other side." Now, when they had left the multitude, they took Him along in the boat as He was. And other little boats were also with Him. And a great windstorm arose, and the waves beat into the boat, so that it was already filling. But He was in the stern, asleep on a pillow. And they awoke Him and said to Him, "Teacher, do You not care that we are perishing?" Then He arose and rebuked the wind, and said to the sea, "Peace, be still!" And the wind ceased and there was a great calm. But He said to them, "Why are you so fearful? How is it that you have no faith?" And they feared exceedingly, and said to one another, "Who can this be, that even the wind and the sea obey Him!" (Mark 4:35-41)

As we go about our daily walk with God, we often think that life will be smooth and never truly believe that anything will hurt us. After all, we are sons and daughters of God, we say.

I have often heard some of God's precious people make all kinds of awkward confessions, mostly in a metaphysical realm. They take a Scripture out of context and claim to stand on it by faith. After pleading and begging with God for a miracle, it never comes. They then become puzzled and feel that God played a trick on them. I believe much of this foolishness is brought in by carnal preachers and teachers in the body of Christ today.

Is there a Red Carpet for Us?

We step into life confident that God has our backs and that every turn will feel like a "red carpet." To some extent, this is true! However, walking with God has never been about our external results as much as our internal growth.

Proverbs 4:18 reads, **"But the path of the just is like the shining sun that shines ever brighter unto the perfect day."** Here is a fact: Our lives grow brighter each day despite what we see happening around us. Our difficult situations, overwhelming temptations, and insecurities all reveal our true condition as human beings and show our deep need for God's provision through His Son, Jesus.

I believe that spiritual growth and ascension (dominion) happen through God's sincere invitations to ride with Him "to the other side." Have you ever been invited to ride with Him?

Riding on the Wings of the Wind!

The Scriptures in Mark 4 show that all the disciples were willing to get on the boat with Jesus and go to the other side. The disciples were so excited about sailing with Jesus that they never thought anything "negative" would come upon them – after all, Jesus was in the boat!

Little did they know that this small ride with Jesus and the intent of crossing over was not just physical but spiritual. The "crossing over to the other side" was about transitioning from several spiritual states. Those states include moving from paralyzing fear to overcoming faith, from pride to contriteness and humility, from arrogance to brokenness, from trying to trust to resting in His tremendous power. What an education!

Whether you and I are willing to admit it or not, our lives are always being challenged to align with God's plan. Whenever we face adversity, it presents an opportunity to strengthen our faith. I also believe each challenge is allowed because God knows we can handle it, not avoid it!

When your heart can honestly tell God, even before the day begins, that you will walk with Him no matter what comes, you are on the path to a great life in God! I will stay close to You, Lord Jesus, through the good, the bad, and the ugly. If you can honestly say this, then you are on your way to a great life in God!

May this bring peace to your soul: It is never about the destination; it's about the valuable lessons you learn and who you become along the way. Remember that the other side isn't just geographical; it's another key to our transformation into the likeness of Christ. Neh'enah.

48

Follow God's Picture for You!

"After these things, the word of the LORD came to Abram in a vision, saying, "Do not be afraid, Abram. I am your shield, your exceedingly great reward." But Abram said, "Lord GOD, what will You give me, seeing I go childless, and the heir of my house is Eliezer of Damascus?" Then Abram said, "Look, you have given me no offspring; indeed, one born in my house is my heir! And behold, the word of the LORD came to him, saying, "This one shall not be your heir, but one who will come from your own body shall be your heir." Then He brought him outside and said, "Look now toward heaven, and count the stars if you are able to number them." And He said to him, "So shall your descendants be." And he believed in the LORD, and He accounted it to him for righteousness." (Genesis 15:1-6)

Living by faith is essential in the kingdom of God. It is the economy of heaven, and not living by faith would mean abandoning all that God has spoken and shown you throughout your journey with Him.

The Bible states that God is Spirit, and when He interacts with man, He speaks to man's inner self or inner man (the spirit man). It is within this realm that God reveals prophetic images of what, where, and how your life can and potentially will turn out if you choose to believe and follow His guidance.

Once we see the picture God has revealed to our hearts, then it is time to act on what He has shown us. A point to note is that when God reveals Himself in our hearts with a vision of our potential future, we must test it with the emotion of peace. If we feel complete peace in our hearts, then it is God. No need to second-guess or doubt – it is the Lord speaking!

In the case of Abram, God had spoken to him in the past. God had promised Abram many descendants. The promise was certain, and the vision was clear, but Abram's outward circumstances told a different story – one of no descendants. Can you see the contrast?

So, what is Abram supposed to do? He did what most of us do. We lower ourselves from the spiritual vision (which God gave him at first) to a natural vision (ruled by outward circumstances). The mistake in this is that we let the "natural" dictate our God-inspired, God-envisioned future.

God's Original Intent Renewed!

Seeing God again is the only solution for our wandering in our journey. Only God Himself can realign us and restore His favor. Abram suggested that Eliezer of Damascus, one of his household servants, be the heir in God's plan. This idea didn't sit well with God: **"And behold, the word of the LORD came to him, saying, "This one shall not be your heir, but one who will come from your own body shall be your heir."**

Once again, God chooses to reveal Himself to Abram and clarify the foggy misunderstanding that had obscured His original intent. Listen to this: "Then He brought him outside and said, **"Look now toward heaven, and count the stars if you are able to number them." And He said to him, "So shall your descendants be."** Once we understand God's intent again, our lives can proceed in the way God has determined, with a clear conscience.

The Scripture says that [Abram] believed in the LORD! I believe we need to reach a point where we fully settle God's vision in our hearts. We must exercise discipline to hear His voice and act accordingly when we face the numerous crossroads on our journey with God. With all that is within you, follow the picture God gave you. Neh'enah.

49

Keep Holding-On Till God Steps In!

"But Moses said to the people, "Do not fear! Stand by and see the salvation of the LORD which He will accomplish for you today; for the Egyptians whom you have seen today, you will never see them again forever. The LORD will fight for you while you keep silent." (Exodus 14:13, 14)

"Listen, all Judah and the inhabitants of Jerusalem and King Jehoshaphat: thus says the LORD to you, 'Do not fear or be dismayed because of this great multitude, for the battle is not yours but God's." (2 Chronicles 20:15)

"When the enemy shall come in like a flood, the Spirit of the LORD shall lift up a standard against him." (Isaiah 59:19b)

Regarding spiritual warfare, the believer must never forget that God empowers us from within and greatly favors us against all our enemies. Although the battle is ongoing, and it will continue, God always raises a standard against the enemy.

When everything appears to be going wrong, God will provide supernatural resources such as favor, grace, and the ability to overcome all opposition. In the end, He will be the only ONE standing.

A Heavenly Perspective!

One thing I have learned in my short walk with God is this heavenly perspective. Heavenly perspective simply means seeing life as God sees it or viewing life from God's point of view.

We have an earthly perspective that influences our decisions based on what we naturally know, see, and hear. For example, we might notice with our natural eyes that things are deteriorating for us. In natural terms, we feel we're about to face some extreme situation. Some call this having common sense, and to some extent, that's true. Please understand we're not abandoning common sense; we're simply inviting God's perspective into our natural view. Do you see what I mean?

Now, when God's heavenly perspective is invited into our dilemma, everything changes. Colossians 3:1-4 talks about us believers being hidden in Christ and in God. We hide behind Christ. Having a heavenly perspective means this: We hide behind Jesus! As the Lord reveals what is happening in our natural world, our earthly perspective shifts. We then see the "bigger picture," as some call it. Do you see this? I pray you do.

Last week, I had a prophetic dream that boosted my faith, and I believe it will do the same for you.

My dream took place in a basketball gym where I was playing a one-on-one game with someone I didn't know. He seemed awkward to me, almost like someone from another planet. One of us shot the ball, and we went for the rebound—both of us grabbing the ball with one hand and fighting for it, but neither of us gave it up. So, we decided to restart the game. When we began the second game, someone shot the ball, and it bounced off the rim. We jumped for the rebound, and the same thing happened again. We grabbed the loose ball with one hand and fought for it, but neither of us yielded. I remember thinking, "He is going to tear the ball out of my hand, and I'm going to lose!" I kept holding on, and so did he. Suddenly, he let go of the ball just when I thought I'd lose it. He started holding his hand in pain, and his arm began turning white. I asked him, "Can I help you?" He replied, "No!" Then he fell to the floor and died. End of dream.

This dream relates to the spiritual battle most believers face every day. Godly decisions, choices, and actions are at the heart of our lives. We must remain committed to choosing to do God's will. Learn to see things from God's heavenly perspective; it requires a deliberate choice.

If you find yourself amid an intense battle, don't let go of the Lord! Don't rely on your own strength, wisdom, or ability. Keep abiding in Him despite what you see or feel. Remember, God will lift a standard against the enemy. When you think you are about to lose, God will step in and deliver you! Neh'enah.

50

The Art of Listening Diligently to the Sound that Instructs!

"For the Lord gives skillful and godly wisdom; from His mouth come knowledge and understanding." (Proverbs 2:6 AMP)

"If you will listen diligently to the voice of the Lord your God, being watchful to do all His commandments which I command you this day, the Lord your God will set you high above all the nations of the earth. And all these blessings shall come upon you and overtake you if you heed the voice of the Lord your God." (Deuteronomy 28:1, 2)

Every secret in life that you and I will ever need to succeed will be found in the secret place of prayer; yes, the secret place of the Highest!

God has reserved wisdom and knowledge for everyone willing to seek it. It has been hidden from the proud but revealed to the broken and contrite. Yes, those who allow themselves to be led by it will lack nothing good. They will enjoy the bounty of the land!

There Is No Voice Like God's Voice!

I want to highlight the following verses in Deuteronomy 28:1, 2.

There is a type of believer who has been shaped and guided by God's voice and will not follow another. These believers walk in confidence, victory, and prosperity all the time. Everything they do and touch seems to turn to gold. Why? Because they have mastered the skill of listening carefully to God's voice.

Now, listening to God's voice is not about hearing poetic lines or rhyming words; it is about the ability to recognize the sound that guides.

When God speaks, it is always to give us instruction. God meets us to guide us, whether through words of wisdom, knowledge, commandments, or precepts. He knows us better than anyone, even ourselves. There will always be our way and His way, and we get to choose which "sound" we will follow.

If we choose to listen to God's voice, the Scripture assures us that "blessings will come upon us and overtake us!" However, if we neglect, ignore, or mock His voice, we will be overtaken by curses caused by our disobedience: **"But if you will not obey the voice of the Lord your God, being watchful to do all His commandments and His statutes which I command you this day, then all these curses shall come upon you and overtake you."** (Deuteronomy 28:15)

I have concluded that if a man or woman of God allows themselves to be taught by God, the results will be significant. These servants have the potential to greatly impact their lives and the lives of others.

Taking the time to learn from God's mouth is a discipline that few have mastered. The past 40 years have shown this in our American culture and society. I dare to say that, as a nation, we are paying a heavy price for it!

Listen, we have only one life to live, and it's very brief. Why not dedicate it to the art of attentively listening to the voice of the Lord and then allowing it to shape us into what He believes is best for us? Neh'enah.

51

The House of God!

"And if the Spirit of Him who raised up Jesus from the dead is dwelling in you, He who raised up Christ from the dead will give Life also to your mortal bodies because of His Spirit who dwells in you." (Romans 8:11 - Weymouth New Testament)

It's amazing how many people have answers for everything when facing this natural life. Whatever a man is missing can be found on Google, in the library, or at your local bookstore.

The section on personal self-development is filled with authors who promise us (if practiced) significant breakthroughs in business, health, dieting, exercise, finances, and more.

Along with self-development, you'll also discover numerous studies across various cultures and sciences, not to mention endless ideas and philosophies in nearly every aspect of practical living.

I must also admit that I have personally taken advantage of these wonderful gifts presented to us in book form by writers around the world. Thousands of years of wisdom and understanding are contained within these pages in black and white. What a blessing to have all of this available to us.

Now, I'm not one to criticize educational principles, especially biblical ones. I have come to value and love the concept of principle-based learning and application. I have also observed both the good and the bad in characters from the Bible. Thank God for the ancient writings: **"For everything that is written from ancient times is written for our teaching, that by patience and by the comfort of the Scriptures we should have**

hope." (Romans 15:4)

I want to share the reality of a spiritual life through this devotional today.

A spiritual life centers on the spirit. Man's spirit resides deep within his innermost being. This is the place where God's Holy Spirit comes to dwell in the human vessel.

It is vital for every servant of God to understand how God's Holy Spirit lives, moves, and exists within.

I opened my devotion to highlighting the great benefits of information from different cultures, sciences, and more, to clearly compare it to what I'm about to show you.

Natural information nourishes man's soul (mind and emotions). Spiritual revelation nourishes the spirit (the innermost being, the house of God) within man.

A hungry and desperate soul cannot find answers by reading books, attending therapy sessions (unless it is a biblical deliverance session), or going to religious services because the soul cannot calm the fierce storm within. Peace can only be given by God through His Spirit into your spirit. All our life issues originate from our spirit and soul.

If we are spirit-led, we will experience life and peace; if we are soulish (fleshly) led, we will experience death. **"For to be carnally minded is death; but to be spiritually minded is life and peace."** (Romans 8:6)

Helping someone with emotional problems without God's Spirit is ineffective. Basically, that person doesn't truly have emotional issues; they are trapped by a lack of spiritual power and revelation. When they allow God's Spirit to come in, dwell, and take control, they will be set free!

General information can assist us in decision-making, during our distress, or in building relationships. However, there will be times when, unless the Spirit of God stirs within us with a fresh revelation of Christ, we cannot experience joy and peace.

Being in the house of God means being in Christ. To be in Christ means that, through our willing choice, He has entered our hearts by the Holy Spirit; we have allowed Him in, and now we are the house of God.

In closing, always prioritize caring for your spirit (God's house) first, then your soul (mind), and finally your body, God's temple. Wisdom advises, "Don't neglect any of these!" Neh'enah.

52

As You Go!

"Now it happened as He went to Jerusalem that He passed through the midst of Samaria and Galilee. Then as He entered a certain village, there met Him ten men who were lepers, who stood afar off. And they lifted up their voices and said, "Jesus, Master, have mercy on us!" So, when He saw them, He said to them, "Go, show yourselves to the priests." And so it was that as they went, they were cleansed." (Luke 17:11-14)

When I think of these ten lepers meeting Jesus in this village, I am moved by the significance of this incredible miracle. For us today, this story provides a model for pursuing our goals and witnessing the results.

Please remember this sacred statement and let it sink into your deepest self: And so, it was that as they went, they were cleansed. Did you catch that? Can you see it? The thing at hand, in this case, the leprosy, left their bodies as they went to show themselves to the priest.

So, it's safe to say that miracles come from obedience. Follow your spirit! Through this devotion, I want to talk about obeying our inner longing.

Obeying the Heart of God!

Many things "call out," but not all will be made manifest. We will have many ideas, but most will fall "by the wayside." It is not the one who dreams big who gets the dream; it is usually the one who gets up after dreaming and takes baby steps toward the dream. He will be sitting with kings!

In my life, I've met a few people with big dreams and visions: people with passion and purpose to change their world, along with many desires and goals. Yet, despite the fire in their hearts, many of those dreams stay only dreams. Why?

Before I share my feelings on this issue and go into more detail, let me first reveal a sobering reality that I have personally witnessed and continue to see every day...

Near my ministry base, there is one of the most significant cemeteries in our region. During prayer times, I often walk by this cemetery. As I walk and pray, I start to think about how many people (who are now buried) fulfilled their dreams.

There are people of all ages and races, and all of them have dreams – some fulfilled, others not! I wouldn't want to leave this world with my dreams buried in the ground, would you?

Attentively Listen!

You can have a great philosophy of life, but if you don't live it, you won't succeed! You can have all the revelations about how something works or should work, but if you don't act, nothing will happen!

You might even have insight into raising a family, making long-lasting friends, raising money, owning your own business, manuals on how to play an instrument, and books on becoming more influential. Still, you won't get anywhere if you don't practice or act on the information provided! The dream will not come true!

Here is what I have discovered: The magic [the miracle] begins to manifest as we dare to walk out the dream we have inside! If you start to practice your dream, the magic kicks in, and things begin to fall into place! As you practice step by step, a formation starts to come together, and you are, without doubt, on your way! In acting, you begin to see the beauty of your dream!

In your plan to fulfill your dream, include some costs for setbacks (it's wise to expect them), but don't let that discourage you. Allow yourself to experience some "heartbreaks" along the way; you'll be just fine! Just stay determined and keep moving forward.

Let your dream transform you into a better person. Let it add value to your life through the challenges you face. Keep moving toward the dream—don't stop! Even if you have to crawl your way there, do it! I'd rather inch my way forward than live with regret for not pushing ahead and not pushing through!

A Word of Caution!

In 1994, roughly 30 years ago, my mentor taught me one of the greatest lessons about trusting God regardless of how things looked on the "outside" – let me share this insight:

We had recently gone through a major church division and split at our local ministry, and things were getting tight, especially regarding finances, Christian workers and helpers, and support in general. The morale of our ministry was very low, and honestly, jumping ship never seemed more tempting.

As we gathered for prayer that early morning at 5 am, the Spirit of the Lord spoke to our senior pastor, our leader, with some prophetic words of comfort. He then called me into his office and, with tears in his eyes, said to me, *"David, the Lord showed me that we are to stay the course. Though the waves seem big for our little ship, we must continue facing them. To turn around at these heights would only flip our boat over as we try to turn around. We must face the waves."* He also added, *"The Lord assured me that the shortest way out of a storm is to go through it, not turn around and go back!*" We stayed the course, and it wasn't long before the storm passed us. To God be the glory now and forever!

Don't stop believing in what you hold inside. It's God's plan for you! May His vision guide your spirit! Neh'enah.

For more books written by David Mayorga, please visit:

www.shabarpublications.com

www.ingramcontent.com/pod-product-compliance
Lightning Source LLC
Chambersburg PA
CBHW021828090426
42811CB00032B/2064/J